M000283482

With New Testament eyes

With New Testament eyes

Pictures of Christ in the Old Testament

Psalms to Malachi

Henry T. Mahan

 EVANGELICAL PRESS

EVANGELICAL PRESS
12 Wooler Street, Darlington, Co. Durham, DL1 1RQ, England

© Evangelical Press 1995
First published 1995

British Library Cataloguing in Publication Data available

ISBN 0 85234 330 2

Scripture quotations in this publication are from the Authorized (King James) Version.

Printed and bound in Great Britain at the Bath Press, Avon.

Contents

1. The psalm of Messiah the King

Psalm 2

The subject of this psalm is the establishment of David upon the throne of Israel, notwithstanding the opposition by his enemies. But the eye of faith will clearly see that this is 'the psalm of Messiah the King', and it sets forth the rage of the wicked against the Lord's anointed, the purpose of God to exalt his own Son and the ultimate reign of Christ over all his enemies. The psalm is best understood under these four heads.

1. An evil conspiracy of demons and men to reject the rule of God

vv.1-3. 'We will be our own god! We will rid ourselves of all restraint and be free to commit all manner of abomination.' What a vain and foolish thing!

Yet *Satan* tried it (Isa. 14:12-15). 'O son of the morning, O day star, how has mischief entered thine heart, to rid thyself of God?' What a vain and empty scheme!

And *Adam* tried it (Gen. 3:5-6). This was the first man's sin: 'We will be gods ourselves,' thereby rejecting the reign and the rule of the Lord God.

Men tried it *at Calvary* (Acts 4:25-28). 'We will not have this man reign over us. We have no king but Cæsar. Crucify him!'

The conspiracy, led by the Antichrist Satan, *continues today* from pulpit and pew to deny and destroy the sovereign Christ (2 Cor. 11:3-4,13-15) and enthrone the human will. 'The will of God must wait upon the will of the creature. God wills to save,' they say, 'and wants to enthrone and exalt Christ, but he has done all that he can do and must depend on the co-operation of man to realize his purpose.' How vain and foolish this is, in the light of the Holy Scriptures! (Exod. 33:18-19; Ps. 135:5-6; Isa. 46:9-11; Eph. 1:5,11). Salvation and eternal life depend solely on the will of God, not the will of men (John 1:11-13; Rom. 9:15-16; James 1:18; John 5:40; Ps. 110:3). Our God is God and King over creation, providence and salvation, and all the organized efforts of foolish, religious men will not alter that fact (John 6:37-39; Rom. 8:28-31).

2. The Lord God will mock his enemies

vv.4-6. **'He that sitteth in the heavens.'** The Lord God is not alarmed over the tumult and mutiny of the earth. 'He sitteth' (his purpose and work completed through his own obedience and death) in the heavens (on a throne of absolute sovereignty) and laughs. Mark the quiet dignity of the omnipotent God. He does not take the trouble to rise up and do battle with the raging people. He laughs! How absurd, how irrational, how futile are the claims and boastings of weak and frail creatures against him!

'**Then** [in his own good time] **shall he speak.'** He does not have to lift his hand nor move from his throne. He only has to speak. He does not speak in compromise or co-operation, but in wrath. Despite your ambitions, despite the wisdom of your counsels, despite the malice of your hearts and despite the unanimous opinion of all earth and hell, **'Yet have I set my king upon my holy hill of Zion.'** Jesus Christ is King of kings and Lord of lords. All things are delivered into his hands. All power over all flesh is his. All authority is given unto him in heaven and earth. The Son gives life to whom he will. He will not fail and the pleasure of the Lord will prosper in his hands. God's anointed is appointed and will not be disappointed! (Phil. 2:9-11). You may rage, you may resolve, you may take counsel and you may boast of the power of your will; but Jesus Christ is King by decree, by design and by death. God's will shall be done (Dan. 4:34-35).

3. The Son himself proclaims the decree

vv. 7-9. We have looked at the counsel of the wicked and heard their raving and boasting. We have looked to the throne of God and observed his infinite power, wisdom and unperturbed counsel and decree: **'Yet have I set my king upon my holy hill of Zion.'** Now Christ, the anointed, risen Redeemer, himself comes forward and says, **'I will declare the decree.'**

'**The Lord hath said unto me, Thou art my Son; this day have I begotten thee.**' He is the true, proper, eternal and only begotten Son of God, declared, owned and acknowledged by Jehovah, the Father (Heb. 1:3-5). 'This day' refers to eternity, which is one continuous day, an everlasting 'now' (Isa. 43:11-13).

'**Ask of me and I shall give thee...**' It was the custom of great kings to give to favoured ones whatever they might ask, so the Lord Jesus has but to ask and he shall have. God, the Father, has promised to uphold our blessed surety and substitute in all his conflicts (Isa. 42:1), yet he prayed for his own (John 17). A seed is promised to him and victory over his enemies, yet for both he prayed.

'**I shall give thee the heathen** [God's elect among the Gentiles] **for thine inheritance,**' and his kingdom will extend to '**the uttermost parts of the earth**' (Rev. 5:9-10). The stubborn and rebellious, who will not have Christ to reign over them, nor bow to his crown rights, he will crush and destroy.

4. Advice is given to all to yield worship and obedience to the Lord's anointed

vv.10-12. '**Be wise ... be instructed.**' It is always wise to be willing to be taught, especially when the Lord speaks and his instructions relate to his glory and the salvation of our very souls. '**Serve the Lord with fear, and rejoice with trembling.**' Let reverence and humility be mingled with your service, that you be not presumptuous, for Christ is a great God and we are puny creatures. But God mingles rejoicing with fear, that obedience may not be slavish. '**Kiss the Son,**' in love, faith and submission. Put aside all doubt, resistance and rebellion and embrace him as Lord and King. They are blessed who put their trust in him.

2. God's two great books

Psalm 19

David devoted himself to the study of God's two great books: the book of *nature*, **'The heavens declare the glory of God'** (v.1); and the book of *Holy Scripture*, **'The law** [the word or doctrine] **of the Lord is perfect'** (v.7). How foolish are those who spend their time and wits trying to resolve discrepancies and contradictions, instead of accepting these two sacred volumes and coming to know the Author! (Rom. 1:18-20; John 20:31). I appreciate the man who is a student of both the world-book and the word-book and can say, 'My Father wrote them both.' Creation and the Scriptures have one author, the living God, and one objective, the glory of God! Creation is the outer court where we look, admire and adore our God (Ps. 8:3-4), and the Word of God is the inner court, where we kneel, worship and praise him (Ps. 119:9-12).

This psalm may be divided into three parts:

vv.1-6.   The creation shows God's glory.
vv.7-11.   The Word reveals God's grace.
vv.12-14. The prayer of the man who understands both.

1. The heavens declare the glory of God

v.1. The heavens are three. There is the third heaven spoken of by Paul in 2 Corinthians 12:2-4. There is the heaven of stars, sun and planets and there is the heaven above the earth with clouds. All are constantly declaring the glory of God and showing his handiwork. If every preacher on earth were silent and every tongue still, the heavens above would never cease to declare the wisdom, power and majesty of our God.

v.2. **'Day unto day uttereth speech.'** Where one day leaves off, the next day takes up the sermon. The day speaks of 'Christ, the light of the world'. The rising sun declares, 'The Sun of righteousness arises with healing in his wings' (Mal. 4:2). While the night speaks of his rest, it also declares, 'I must work ... while it is day, for the night cometh when no man can work' (John 9:4). There will come an eternal day and eternal darkness. The passing of day and night speaks of the brevity of life. 'Teach us to number our days that we may apply our hearts unto wisdom' (Ps. 90:12).

v.3. Many are the languages of men on earth; but there is no speech nor language on earth where the voice of God's heavens is not heard, for the teaching of creation is not directed to the ear but to the eye and heart. 'God hath showed it unto them' (Rom. 1:19).

v.4. The teaching and instructions of God's creation have gone out through all the earth. No man living beneath the heavens is beyond the reach of God's outer court preacher. **'In the heavens God has made a tabernacle for the sun.'** Like a mighty king, the sun continues on its way, attended by the moon and the stars.

vv.5-6. Who is meant by this sun? It is a picture of our Lord Jesus Christ — the Sun of righteousness!

Jesus Christ, like the sun, is the centre, light and life of God's new creation (Rev. 21:23).

Jesus Christ, like the sun, dwells in the midst of revelation. He tabernacled among men in all his brightness. All that was made was made by him and for him, and by him it is held together (Col. 1:16-17).

Jesus Christ comes forth as the Bridegroom of his elect church.

Jesus Christ rejoices as the strong man who wins the battle over the forces of evil and death (Isa. 53:10-12).

His going forth is from everlasting to everlasting (Micah 5:2). His circuit of mercies blesses the farthest ends and remotest corners of the earth (Rev. 5:9).

There are none who believe who shall be denied the warmth and comfort of his love, and none who do not believe who shall escape the heat of his wrath.

2. The Word of God reveals his grace

v.7.   **'The law of the Lord is perfect, converting the soul.'** This is not the law of Moses, but the whole text of Holy Scripture. The great means of conversion is the Word of God (Rom. 10:13-17; James 1:18; 1 Peter 1:23; Rom. 1:16-17). **'The testimony of the Lord is sure, making wise the simple.'** What God has to say in his Word about himself, his dear Son, our sin and salvation is sure, certain and infallible (1 John 5:10-13). Humble, teachable minds receive the Word of God and are made wise unto salvation (1 Cor. 2:8-10).

v.8.   **'The statutes of the Lord are right, rejoicing the heart.'** The statutes of the Lord are his counsel and decrees. His covenant of mercy and grace and these statutes are founded in righteousness. God will be just and justifier! God will be righteous and merciful (Ps. 85:10; Isa. 45:21; Rom. 3:25-26). These righteous decrees rejoice the hearts of those taught of God. There is a reason for rejoicing when one understands how that in Christ, God can redeem us and still be God! **'The commandment of the Lord is pure, enlightening the eyes.'** The pure, holy Word of God (who will by no means clear the guilty) is revealed to us in Christ Jesus and our eyes are opened to his glory (2 Cor. 4:3-6).

v.9. **'The** [reverent] **fear of the Lord is clean, enduring for ever.'** Still the Word of God is intended, which teaches men an awe, a reverent fear and the worship of God. The Word of God directs us to the blood of Christ, which cleanses us from all sin and fear of the curse and leaves us only to love and worship our God. While the ceremonial law is done away, the gospel is for ever.

vv.10-11. **'The judgements of the Lord are true and righteous altogether.'** His decrees, his covenant, his mercies and his condemnations are founded on truth and righteousness. They shall stand and bring both riches and pleasure to all who believe. By hearing them a man is warned and by obeying them a man is greatly rewarded.

3. The prayer of the man who can read the two books

vv.12-14. The man who knows God and his Word knows himself. 'Cleanse me from sins which even I do not see. Keep me from presuming on the mercy of God. Let not the flesh have dominion over me, and deliver me from apostasy and departing from the living God. Let my words praise God, speak peace to my brother, be free from malice and murmuring. Let the meditations of my heart be sincere, submissive to thy will, and dwell much on Christ.'

3. The psalm of the cross

Psalm 22

Mr Spurgeon said of this psalm, 'This psalm may have been actually repeated word by word by our Lord when hanging on the tree. It begins with "My God, my God, why hast thou forsaken me?" and ends, according to some, in the original with "It is finished." David and his afflictions may be here in a very modified sense; but, as the star is concealed by the light of the sun, he who sees the Lord Jesus will probably neither see nor care to see David. Before us, in this psalm, we have a description both of the darkness and of the glory of the cross — the sufferings of Christ and the glory which shall follow.'

v.1. What is the one great cause why God should forsake his Son at such a time? There was no cause in him. Why then was he forsaken? Christ was our substitute, who was numbered with the transgressors and who bore our sins in his own body. He endured our death, judgement and hell, being separated from God for a time.

v.2. Our Lord prayed in the daytime of life and in the night season of death. Our Lord prayed when he was heard and even in this dark hour of desertion, when he was not heard. He believed perfectly for us, his elect.

v.3. Our Lord seems to marvel (as do all who know that the Father and Son are one) how the holy God could forsake him and be silent to his cries. But the argument is: **'Thou art holy.'** His mercy, love and grace are seen in God's giving his Son to die for us and the holiness of God is seen in the forsaking of Christ. God must be just and holy, even in the expression of his love.

vv.4-5. Our Lord pleads the past dealings of God with his people. Three times he says, **'They trusted'**, and never left off trusting and were not put to shame. They trusted Jehovah (God our Saviour), who in Christ will always hear. The plural pronoun *'our* **fathers'** shows Christ's oneness with them and us.

v.6. **'I am a worm.'** What abasement! What a miracle! What a contrast between 'I AM' and 'I am a worm'! He was made lower than the angels (Ps. 8:4-5), in the form of a servant, identified with Jacob, the worm (Isa. 41:14; Mal. 3:6). He was forsaken that we might be accepted (Eph. 1:6).

vv.7-8. Our Lord endured every cruelty, scorn and insult. Not only did he bear the wrath of God, but the contempt of man. Read the account in Matthew 27:39-44 and note the five different ways in which taunts were hurled at Christ in these verses.

vv.9-10. The Son of Man was marvellously begotten of the Holy Spirit (Luke 1:34-35). God prepared a body for him (Heb. 10:5-7). From the womb he was God incarnate, the sinner's hope, and he knew from the very beginning that his mission was sure and secure (John 6:37-39).

v.11. Our Lord's great woe was that God had forsaken him; his great prayer was that God would sustain him even in this hour. **'There is none to help.'** He must tread the winepress alone, 'by himself purge our sins' and, being a man, must have divine help. Our Lord is the Lamb slain from the beginning, but he must die! Our Lord has a people, but he must pray for them! Our Lord has all power, but as our substitute he prays for the divine presence.

vv.12-13. The mighty ones in the crowd are meant. The priests, Pharisees, rulers and captains all surrounded the cross of this naked, rejected one, mocking him.

vv.14-17. Our Lord describes his condition and suffering. His greatest agony and suffering were soul miseries (Isa. 53:10-11), but the death of the cross was indescribable agony. He was utterly spent, like water poured out on the ground. The intense pain made his heart to feel like wax melted in the heat. His strength and moisture were dried up and his tongue swollen with thirst. They drove nails into his hands and feet and he was so stretched upon the cross that one could see all his bones against the skin, pulled out of joint.

v.18. Every act of the wicked men at Calvary was prophesied in Scripture (Matt. 27:35; Acts 4:26-28; 13:29-30).

vv.19-21. Oh, what a perfect Saviour! 'Having loved his own, he loved them to the end,' and even in his lowest hour of suffering, he wants nothing but his God. **'O Lord: O my strength, haste thee to help me. Deliver my soul from the sword** [Zech. 13:7]**; my darling from the power of the dog.'** Was not this prayer for us, his own? (John 17).

vv.22-31. Here in these verses is the foretaste of deliverance and victory! Our Redeemer beholds the glory of his triumph and the results of his suffering and rejoices (Isa. 53:11-12).

'I will declare thy name unto my brethren.' He speaks here of his church. He is not ashamed to call them brethren (Heb. 2:10-12).

'The seed of Israel' is all believers (Gal. 3:7,29).

'All the ends of the world ... and all the kindreds of the nations shall worship thee.' Our Lord has a people of every nation (Rev. 5:9).

They shall come from all parts, those who are born of God, and declare *his* righteousness, and it shall be said: 'The Lord hath done this!'

4. 'The Lord is my Shepherd'

Psalm 23

Many have tried to determine when David wrote this psalm. Was it when he was a shepherd? Or when he fled from Saul? Or when he was peacefully settled on Israel's throne? Or when he was in the sunset years and contemplated the eternal house of the Lord? No one knows, but in the Scriptures it follows the 22nd Psalm, which is 'the psalm of the cross'. It is only after we have read and understood, 'My God, my God, why hast thou forsaken me?' that we can truthfully say, 'The Lord is my Shepherd.' The Lord must purchase the sheep of whom he is the Shepherd (John 10:14-18).

v.1. **'*The Lord* [Jesus Christ] is my shepherd.'** He is the Lord of lords and King of kings. His lordship is based on his ownership (John 3:35; Col. 1:16-18). He is Lord by divine decree (Ps. 2:6-7; Heb. 1:2; Phil. 2:9-11). He is Lord by death (Rom. 14:9). He is my Lord now by faith (Rom. 10:9-10).

'The Lord [Jesus Christ] *is my shepherd.'* He *is* (no if, maybe, or perhaps about it) *my* Shepherd. He owns me, for the Father gave me to him from all eternity (John 6:37-39). He loves me and bought me by his blood (1 Cor. 6:20). He is the Great Shepherd of the sheep (Heb. 13:20). He is the Chief Shepherd (1 Peter 5:4). He is the Good Shepherd (John 10:11).

'I shall not want.' I may be the weakest of the sheep, but I shall not want! I may be the most stupid, I may wander and stray, I may grow old and feeble — but I shall not want! I may not have all that I wish, but I shall not want! I may endure sickness and sorrow, walk the valley of death and stand before God's awful throne — but I shall not want, for the Lord is my Shepherd! I shall not want for any good thing, for he is able to save (Heb. 7:25). He is able to keep that which I have committed to him (2 Tim. 1:12). He is able to present me faultless before the throne (Jude 24-25), and he is able to raise my vile body in that day (Phil. 3:20-21).

v.2.   I shall not want for *rest*, for **'He maketh me to lie down in green pastures.'** I have no reason to be fearful, nor afraid of my enemies, of the curse of the law, or of death and judgement. I need not stand ready to flee, but can lie down in the green pastures of his Word and rest (Matt. 11:28-29).

I shall not want for *peace*, for **'He leadeth me beside the still waters.'** Our lives are made up of two parts: thoughts and deeds, or meditation and activity. Blessed is the person who can say in both areas, 'The Lord is my Shepherd.' I rest in my mind and soul, fed by his Word and assured by his promises, and I walk beside calm waters. Trials of life are pictured as deep waters, troubled waters and waves of the sea, but my Shepherd has calmed the troubled sea and even trials are for my good (Rom. 8:28).

v.3.   I shall not want for *redemption* and *forgiveness*, for **'He restoreth my soul.'** He restored it to life, for in Adam I died (1 Cor. 15:21-22). He restored it to purity (Rom. 5:19). He restored it to God (2 Cor. 5:19). He will restore my soul and body to power and glory to reign with him (1 Cor. 15:51-57).

'He leadeth me in paths of righteousness for his name's sake.' It is not my nature to know the path of righteousness, nor to find it, nor to recognize it, nor to walk therein. But he leads me there, for it is his path. He made me righteous before God and leads me in that path, both to love it and to walk in it (Rom. 3:21-26; 10:1-4). He leads me in paths of righteousness 'for his name's sake'; that is, for his glory and the praise of his grace (Eph. 1:6,12,14). I shall not want for *holiness*.

v.4.   I shall not want for *companionship* or *comfort*, for **'Thou art with me,'** and **'Thy rod and staff they comfort me.'** Almost everyone applies **'the valley of the shadow of death'** to the time of physical death, but I believe this valley of death through which we walk is our entire journey through this world. It is called a valley of *death* because the fall of Adam put the stamp of death on everything here; we are *walking through* this world; it is not our dwelling-place; and it is called the *shadow* of death because Christ has removed the substance of death and only a shadow remains. A shadow is there but cannot hurt or destroy.

'I will fear no evil.' He does not say the evil is not there; it is, but we do not fear because Christ is with us! Where the sheep are, the Shepherd is! 'Lo, I am with you always.'

Some say 'the rod and staff' are correction and chastisement, which is surely a comfort, for 'Whom the Lord loveth he chasteneth' (Heb. 12:6-7). Some say the rod and staff are for numbering the sheep as they pass underneath. Others say the rod and staff are symbols of his sovereignty, direction and defence. He rules the flock, defends the flock and directs the flock where he would have them go. Perhaps all are meant, for all are comforting.

v.5. I shall not want for *provisions*, even in the presence of my enemies, for my Shepherd will supply all my needs (Phil. 4:19). The believer is not without enemies (Eph. 6:12). He would not be like his Lord if he did not have enemies (John 15:17-20). Our enemies are the world, the flesh and the devil, but he fully sets the table and nothing is lacking. There is no hurry, no confusion; we sit down with our Lord and feast as though the enemy did not even exist (Isa. 26:3-4).

v.6. I shall not want for *anything in this life nor in the life to come*, for his **'goodness and mercy shall follow me all the days of my life: and I will dwell in the house of the Lord for ever'**. This is neither presumption nor a claim to personal worth or merit. It is faith and confidence in the Lord Jesus, who is the Great Shepherd, the Chief Shepherd and the Good Shepherd.

5. True God, true Israel, true Redeemer

Psalm 24

This psalm is more appreciated and best understood if it is divided into three sections:

1. The true God (vv.1-2).
2. The true Israel (vv.3-6).
3. The true Redeemer (vv.7-10).

1. The true God

v.1. **'The earth is the Lord's.'** The earth is not man's; it is the Lord's! Men may live on earth and boast of their possessions and power. They may divide the earth into countries, fly their flags and elect their kings and rulers. They may divide these countries into states and provinces and give them names. They may divide these provinces into farms, estates and allotments and issue title-deeds of ownership. But the earth is not man's; it is the Lord's. 'Whatsoever is under the whole heaven is mine' (Job 41:11).We are only tenants, subject to eviction at any moment. The great landowner sits in the heavens and laughs at the title-deeds of the worms in the dust.

'The earth is the Lord's, and the fulness thereof.' The 'fulness' of the earth may mean its entirety — its wealth, its life, its past, present and future. The Lord has made the earth to be full and he keeps it full. The air is full, notwithstanding all who breathe it. The soil is full, though billions of plants, trees and flowers derive their nourishment from it. The rivers, forests and fields remain full to feed, clothe and house generations of people. They are all full and held together by his sovereign hand (Col. 1:16-17).

'The world, and they that dwell therein.' All that dwell upon the earth and live in his world belong to the Lord Jesus Christ.

They are his by creation (John 1:1-3; Rev. 4:11).

They are his by decree; the Father has given him all things (John 3:35; 17:2; Heb. 1:2).

They are his by purchase (Rom. 14:9).

They are his by administration; he reigns (Matt. 28:18; Isa. 9:6).

All creatures are his — either his sons or his servants, his sheep or his goats, his vessels of mercy or his vessels of wrath; but they are his!

v.2. **'He hath founded it upon the seas.'** Here is the chief reason all this is his — he created it all (Gen. 1:1-31). It was God who said, 'Let the dry land appear... Let us make man.'

He **'established it upon the floods'** — the waters above and beneath the earth. What an insecure foundation! Surely God is saying that the earth will not remain. We look forward to a new heaven and a new earth founded on the 'Rock of ages', where there will be 'no more sea' (Rev. 21:1). Oh, the power, glory, majesty and greatness of our God! (Ps. 50:10-12).

2. The true Israel

vv.3-6. **'Who shall ascend into the hill of the Lord?'** Oh, how high above us is our God! He dwells in the heavens (Eccles. 5:1-2; Job 11:7-8), in the light which no man can approach (1 Tim. 6:16).

'Who shall stand in his holy place?' If anyone could ascend to where God dwells, who could stand, or abide, in his presence? The answer is fourfold:

'He that hath clean hands' — one who has never sinned.

'And a pure heart' — one who has not even imagined or thought any evil thought .

'Who hath not lifted up his soul unto vanity' — one who has loved God perfectly and done nothing contrary to God.

'Nor sworn deceitfully' — one who is and has spoken perfect truth.

These conditions suit none but Jesus Christ! Therefore, no man has ascended to heaven, nor will ascend to heaven, nor stand in his

holy place, except he who came down from heaven — 'the Son of
man which is in heaven' (John 3:13). Christ, the God-man, met
every condition as our representative, and we shall ascend and we
shall stand and we shall dwell in the presence of the Lord, accepted
in the Beloved (Eph. 1:6; Col. 1:21-22; Jude 24-25). As Christ has
been raised from the dead and has been blessed, so in him we shall
'receive the blessing' of the presence of **'the Lord, and righteousness from the God of his salvation'** (v.5).

'This is the generation of them that seek him [Christ]**, that
seek thy face, O** [God of] **Jacob'** (v.6). Heaven is populated by
'seekers and finders'. By his grace they seek the Lord, his presence,
his mercy, his righteousness in Christ, and they find in him all they
need. This is the true Israel (Phil. 3:3) from every nation.

3. The true Redeemer

vv.7-10. Jesus Christ, our Lord, answered to the full character laid
down for those who would ascend to the hill of the Lord and stand
in his presence! By his own right and righteousness he has entered
in and sat down at the Father's right hand (Heb. 1:3). His hands are
clean, his heart is pure, his soul loves God perfectly and he is the
truth! Therefore, **'Lift up your heads, O ye gates; and be ye lift up,
ye everlasting doors.'** The gates and doors of eternal glory have
always been closed to men; too many things prevent them from
entering. But the Son of Man has come to earth; his perfect work of
redemption is done. 'It is finished,' he cried. 'Now open, ye gates
and doors, to the King of glory and his church.'

'Who is this King of glory?' He is **'the Lord strong and
mighty'**, able to do all that he undertakes (Heb. 7:25). He is **'the
Lord mighty in battle'**, for he alone conquered every enemy. He is
'the Lord of hosts'. He came alone to redeem, but he is not alone
when he ascends: he has with him a number which no man can
number. He is **'the King of glory'**. All glory is his, in him and of
him.

6. Eight great precepts

Psalm 37

The author of this psalm is David, the time of its writing is in his old age (v.25) and the subject has to do with the prosperity of the wicked while the people of God suffer affliction and trial. This has troubled and perplexed many, as indicated in Psalm 73. This is a psalm in which the Lord sweetly hushes the complaints of his people and calms their minds concerning his present dealings with them.

Briefly, here are some of the questions raised and answered:

vv.1-2. Evil-doers flourish and prosper like the green grass and the green herb, but they shall soon be cut down and wither like the grass (Isa. 40:6-8).

vv.12-13. The wicked hate believers and persecute them, yet the Lord laughs at their opposition (Ps. 2:4), for their day of judgement is coming (Deut. 32:35).

vv.14-15. The wicked take advantage of believers and draw their swords to hurt them, but their swords shall enter their own hearts.

vv.16-17. Believers seem to have so little, while great are the riches of wicked men, but their riches are temporary and shall fade, while our inheritance is for ever.

v.20. The enemies of the Lord seem to get fatter and fatter, but it is the fat of 'lambs for the slaughter'. Who envies the pig or the turkey which is well fed while being prepared for the slaughter?

vv.35-37. The wicked on earth have great power and proudly flaunt that power and greatness like a great tree, but they shall soon pass away and no remembrance of them can be found. Mark the believer in Christ; his end is eternal peace.

vv.38-40. What is the bottom line? Where is all this settled? How are we to be comforted in our trials, while we watch the wicked prosper, flourish and live in ease? Look at their destruction and final condemnation (Ps. 73:12-17), then look at the grace of God to believers in Christ!

> 1. Grace is described — **'The salvation of the righteous is of the Lord.'**
> 2. Grace is summarized — The Lord is our **'strength'** and he will **'deliver'** us.
> 3. Grace is characterized — **'They trust in him.'**

In the light of all that has been said, David lays down eight great precepts or directions for God's people.

1. **'Fret not thyself because of evildoers'** (v.1). Do not burn with jealousy, envy or anger over the prosperity of wicked men; they have all now that they shall ever have. They spend their brief days upon earth in ease and riches, but they shall soon be cut down like the weeds. A sight of their terrible end ought to deliver us from envying them, and were it not for God's grace and our Lord's redemption, we would be among them.

2. **'Trust in the Lord'** (v.3). Faith in Christ will cure fretting. Our outward conduct depends on our inward attitude and confidence in our God. Trust not men nor riches; they will come to naught (Ps. 146:3-5). Trust in the Lord for pardon, protection, provision and his wise providence. **'Thou shalt be fed'** — supplied with all that is needed (Ps. 37:25; Matt. 6:30-33; Phil. 4:19).

3. **'Delight thyself ... in the Lord'** (v.4). He who is commanded not to fret, he who is commanded to trust, is also exhorted to delight in the Lord. In giving up the world, we have given up nothing! In Christ Jesus we have all spiritual blessings (Eph. 1:3). Like Moses, we know that the reproach of Christ is greater riches than all the treasures of the world (Heb. 11:26). Therefore, we delight in our Lord, we rejoice in him and we are glad to go into the house of the Lord. We delight in the law of the Lord (Ps. 1:2). We delight to do

his will (Ps. 40:8). His mercy and comfort delight our souls (Ps. 94:19). We sit down under his shadow with great delight (S.of S. 2:3). 'Godliness with contentment is great gain' (1 Tim. 6:6).

4. **'Commit thy way unto the Lord'** (v.5). Cast away anxiety, worry and fear: 'Casting all your care upon him; for he careth for you' (1 Peter 5:7). Roll the whole burden of life and eternity upon the Lord, like the farmer who ploughs the field, plants the seed and leaves the harvest to the Lord — for what else can he do? Trust him, for he will bring it to pass.

5. **'Rest in the Lord'** (v.7). When God completed the creation of the world, it is said that he rested. This is not a rest from weariness, but simply a declaration that there was no more to do — creation was finished! Our Lord Jesus entered into his rest, having finished the work of redemption (Heb. 4:10). Let us strive to enter into his rest. Cease from fretting, labouring and doubting, and rest in him (Matt. 11:28-30). The more one learns of his sufficiency, the greater the rest!

6. **'Cease from anger'** (v.8). Knowing the good providence of the Lord and his eternal purpose to accomplish our good (Rom. 8:28), we entertain no anger towards his ways. Knowing the ignorance and blindness of natural men and that God is the first cause of all things, we hold no anger nor hate for them (Gen. 50:19-20). Getting even or getting revenge against men is not for us, but is in God's hands (Heb. 10:30). Anger does not work God's righteousness (James 1:19-20).

7. **'Depart from evil'** (v.27). Here is a double precept: 'Depart from evil,' from the world, the flesh and the devil, and **'do good'**. Work the works of righteousness and honesty and adorn the gospel of the Lord Jesus with good works, that men may glorify our Father in heaven.

8. **'Wait on the Lord'** (v.34). He who truly trusts in the Lord and delights in the Lord will rest in the Lord and wait on God's time for all things. Do not bind God to a day or a way. Spurgeon said, 'Wait on the Lord in obedience as a servant, wait in hope as an heir and wait in expectation as a believer.' **'He shall exalt thee to inherit the land.'**

7. 'My hope is in thee'

Psalm 39

This is a psalm of David.

1. *A man after God's own heart* (1 Sam. 13:14; Acts 13:22).
2. *A man of activity and affliction.* David was totally committed to God. He was totally involved in God's kingdom, with its warfare, conflicts and glory. You will not find David indifferent to the purpose and providence of God. He was a participant (1 Sam. 17:26-29; Ps. 119:71).
3. *A man of strong passions and feelings.* He loved people, as evidenced by his love for Jonathan and Mephibosheth. He was a humble man, as evidenced by his dancing before the ark (2 Sam. 6:20-23). He praised God (Ps. 150).
4. *A man of strong faith* (Ps. 27:13; 116:10). He never ceased to believe God, whatever the circumstances. God allowed David to write the Messianic psalms, speaking the very words of Christ as though they were his own (Ps. 22).

This psalm was written in a time of great conflict, sorrow and trial, as is indicated by, **'My sorrow was stirred'** (v.2); **'How frail I am'** (v.4); **'Deliver me from all my transgressions'** (v.8); **'Every man is vanity'** (v.11); **'Hold not thy peace at my tears'** (v.11) and **'O spare me, that I may recover strength'** (v.13). Let us listen and learn from this man, so strong in faith, so strong in his passions and yet so tempted and tried.

v.1.   **'I said.'** It was to himself that he spoke. Wise is the man who spends much time meditating and communicating with his own heart (Ps. 4:4; 77:6-12; 2 Cor. 13:5). David was evidently under a strong burden and trial and was afflicted by God. Some of it he did not understand and God had not seen fit to reveal his purpose in it. So David said to himself, **'I will take heed to my ways, that I sin**

not with my tongue.' Like Job of old, he was careful not to charge God foolishly (Job 1:22). The tongue is a small member but capable of great evil, especially when speaking in reference to God and spiritual matters. He continued, 'I will especially put a bridle on my mouth while the unbeliever is before me.' How carefully must our words be chosen at all times, but especially in the presence of those who misuse and misunderstand even the purest of speech! O Lord, for the grace and wisdom to learn this one verse and practise it — to muzzle my mouth and subdue my tongue!

v.2. **'I was dumb with silence, I held my peace, even from** [speaking] **good.'** He is saying, 'I determined, in my affliction, not to speak in complaint or instruction, lest if I begin to talk, I should say things I should not say.' Our world is a world of talkers; no one hesitates to express an opinion, even about the mysteries of God. But David was concerned, not only about murmuring against God, but about speaking carelessly and without inspiration of the good things of God (Eccles. 5:1-2; Job 40:4-5; 42:3); so he resolved to be silent.

v.3. But while he meditated on these things and was resolved neither to speak evil nor good, his heart burned within him and would not let him keep silent. The believing, regenerated heart will not keep still before God, but must cry to God, must praise God, must speak in prayer and communion. 'As [a man] thinketh in his heart, so is he' (Prov. 23:7). It is with the heart that men believe God (Rom. 10:9-10). It is in the heart that the love of God is shed abroad (Rom. 5:5). Newton said, 'Sooner expect a man to live without breathing, as to expect a believer to live without praying.' 'Christ ... is our life,' and 'In everything give thanks' (Col. 3:4; 1 Thess. 5:18).

v.4. There is a threefold request made to God:

1. **'Make me to know mine end,'** the end and perfection of all my desires (Ps. 23:6; 27:4). 'I shall be satisfied, when I awake, with thy likeness' (Ps. 17:15). All things should be judged by their end (Ps. 73:17). In Christ our end, and our goal, is to be like him (1 John 3:2-3).
2. **'Make me to know ... the measure of my days.'** How short they are upon the earth!

3. '**Make me to know ... how frail I am.**' An understanding of my frailty and flesh will make me humble, will make me more diligent about my relationship with Christ Jesus, will make me more patient with others and will wean me from this world of flesh and cause me to trust and rest in Christ.

v.5. '**Thou hast made my days as an handbreadth.**' This is one of the shortest measures. A man does not need a long line to measure a short life. We carry the measure of our days with us. Hold it out and look at it often.

'**Mine age is as nothing before thee.**' My age is short compared to Methuselah's 900 years, but before the eternal God it is nothing (Ps. 90:12).

'**Every man at his best state is altogether vanity.**' The word is 'empty, unprofitable and unsatisfactory'. Men are good only at that which is bad; men are wise only in foolishness; men are consistent only in their inconsistency; at his best moment man is only emptiness.

'**Selah**' means 'Pause, say it again. This is the end of the matter. Amen!'

v.6. The vanity of man at his best state is illustrated in three things.

   1. *The vanity of our joys and honours:* he'**walketh in a vain show**'. The allusion is to a parade where men dress up and act out a borrowed part. We die and someone else acts the part.

   2. *The vanity of our griefs and sorrows:* '**They are disquieted in vain.**' Even our turmoil and distress are for nothing, for time will erase even these.

   3. *The vanity of our possessions:* '**He heapeth up riches.**' He builds a house and a stranger lives in it. He saves money and his sons spend it. He accumulates the chaff of the world and God will burn it.

The world consists of fruitless honour, needless cares and useless riches.

v.7. David thought on all these things of natural life and the world and said, '**What wait I for?**' What is there to enchant me? What is there to enthral me? What is there to interest me? **'My hope is in thee.'** My hope is in the Lord's grace and mercy; my hope is in my Redeemer; my hope is in the atonement on the mercy-seat. In Christ I shall live when all else dies, I shall be full when all else is empty and I shall stand when all else fails!

vv.8-10. **'Deliver me from all my transgressions'** (see Ps. 51:1-5). 'Suffer me not to show impatience in affliction and give the wicked room to reproach. I kept silent in suffering because you gave it to me. Now deliver me.' Afflictions in the lives of his people are sent by God and removed by God.

vv.11-13. God's dealings with us cause us to know our sins and weep over them, and cause our beauty and righteousness to become filthy rags, that we may seek his righteousness in Christ (Rom. 10:1-4).

8. 'Many, O Lord, are thy wonderful works'

Psalm 40:1-10

These are the words of David, for this is a psalm of David, inspired by the Holy Spirit. The words reveal David's faith and experience, which he lived, felt and expressed in a song.

These are the words of the Lord Jesus Christ, as Hebrews 10:5-9 tells us.

Are these words not also the experience of every believer? So complete is our union with Christ that it is impossible to speak of Christ and not speak of his people in the same words (John 17:21-22).

v.1. The psalm begins with a word that is so difficult for us: **'I waited patiently for the Lord,'** or 'Waiting, I waited'. David expected wisdom, direction, provision and strength from the Lord, all of which he gives in his own time; therefore, he was willing to patiently wait on God (Ps. 27:13-14).

'He inclined unto me, and heard my cry.' 'He bent over to me and heard my cry. In the Lord's own time, when the trial had accomplished his design, when I could understand his instructions, when he could get all the glory and praise, when I was sufficiently shut up to his grace, he heard my cry.' It is a marvel that God should condescend to hear us at all. Then why should we ever grow impatient and weary with waiting for him?

vv.2-3. There are three powerful statements here that accurately describe the work of Christ in redeeming his people.

'He brought me up ... out of an horrible pit.' Some of these prison pits in the Bible were deep, with mud and corruption at the bottom and with no possible way out except through a hole at the top. We were in the pit of sin, under the curse of the law, with no way out; and he, according to his own will, by his mercy and grace, came to where we were (John 1:14), paid our debt, restored our souls and lifted us up to light, life and freedom (1 Sam. 2:6-8; Luke 4:18).

'He set my feet upon a rock, and established my goings.' That rock is Christ (1 Cor. 10:4). My steps are set, settled and established on the unchangeable, immovable rock of absolutes in Christ — God's word of promise and God's atonement in Christ (1 Cor. 1:30-31).

'He hath put a new song in my mouth,' which is a song of **'praise unto our God'**. That new song is the song of a new creature in Christ, the song of the new covenant, the song of the new and living way, the song of a new heart and the song of a new heaven and a new earth. This new song is the gospel of Christ by which the Holy Spirit will enable many 'to see, fear and trust the Lord'.

v.4. **'Blessed is the man that maketh the Lord his trust,'** who can say with Job, 'Though he slay me, yet will I trust him,' and with Peter, 'Thou art the Christ, the Son of the living God' and with John, 'We know we have passed from death to life.' A believer may be as persecuted as Job, as poor as Lazarus, as lonely as Elijah, as bowed down as David; but if the Lord is his trust and refuge, none of these outward afflictions shall move him. He does not bow to money or power, nor cringe before worldlings. He is not swayed by the multitudes who run after a lie. God is his refuge and strength, a very present help in trouble.

v.5. The **'wonderful works'** of God are his works of creation, providence, redemption and glorification. George Rogers gave this outline:

> 1. The works of God are planned by God, wrought by his Spirit, through the merits of his Son.
> 2. They are wonderful works in their variety, their fulness and their unchangeable glory.
> 3. They are innumerable, all in perfect order and beyond comprehension.

vv.6-8. Here David goes beyond himself and speaks the very words of Christ. When anyone thinks of 'the wonderful works of God', it is of Christ that he must speak (Col. 1:16-19).

The sacrifices and offerings not desired nor required are the sacrifices offered under the law. These sacrifices could never put away sin, could never please God's justice or righteousness. They were offered from Adam to Moses only as types and shadows of Christ (Heb. 10:1-4). They no longer exist, because Christ has come. **'"In the volume of the book it is written of me,"** that I should come to fulfil all righteousness, honour every attribute and satisfy justice,' says Christ. 'My ear was bored,' for he is a willing servant. **'I delight to do thy will,'** for he is one with the Father. 'The volume of the book' may be both the book of God's eternal counsel and designs (Rev. 5:1-5) and the book of Scripture (Luke 24:44-46).

vv.9-10. The Son has fully and ably declared these five things (Heb. 1:1-3):

1. *God's righteousness*: both his essential righteousness and his righteousness imputed to believers through faith (Rom. 10:1-4; 3:19-26; 4:20-25).

2. *God's faithfulness.* Our God is faithful to his covenant, to his Word, to his Son and to his people (Isa. 46:9-11). 'I am the Lord, I change not' (Mal. 3:6). The gifts and calling of God are without change (Rom. 11:29). 'Known unto God are all his works from the beginning,' and they shall be done (Acts 15:18; John 6:37-39; Rom. 8:29-31).

3. *God's salvation.* Salvation is of the Lord in its origination. Christ is our surety, Saviour and the Lamb slain for us from the beginning. Salvation is of the Lord in its execution: 'It pleased the Lord to bruise him' (Isa. 53:10). Salvation is of the Lord in its application: 'It pleased God ... to reveal his Son in me' (Gal. 1:15-16). Salvation is of the Lord in its sustaining power. We 'are kept by the power of God through faith' (1 Peter 1:5). Salvation is of the Lord in its ultimate glory: He 'hath made us kings and priests' (Rev. 1:6; 5:10; Phil. 3:20-21).

4. *God's lovingkindness.* When the Bible speaks of God's wrath, it is always against sin, and when the Bible speaks of God's love for sinners, it is always in Christ (Rom. 8:38-39; John 3:36; 14:21; 17:23).

5. *God's truth.* Christ is the truth. There is no knowing God except as we learn and know Christ. While God's power, glory and majesty are seen in the creation, the attributes and character of God are only revealed in Christ. His chief glory is his goodness and grace in Christ (Exod. 33:18-19; 2 Cor. 4:3-6).

9. A song of love

Psalm 45

v.1. From the very first words, the psalmist leaves us in no doubt as to the subject of this psalm: 'I speak of things pertaining to the king.' This song has **'the king'**, the Lord Jesus Christ, for its only subject. Therefore, it is indeed **'a good matter'**: good, because 'Only God is good', and he speaks of Christ, who is the chief good; good for us, because the gospel of Christ is good news to sinners (Luke 2:10-11). He says, 'My heart is bubbling up,' full and running over with his glory; therefore, my tongue is ready to put into words my love for him, his love for me and the truth concerning his person and work.

v.2. As though the King himself had appeared before him, the psalmist, full of admiration and devotion, addresses his Lord: **'Thou art fairer than the children of men.'** We are born; he is the only begotten Son. We are children of dust; he is the Lord from heaven. We are darkness; he is light. We are empty; in him dwells all fulness. **'Grace is poured into thy lips.'** Grace is treasured up in him and he is the fountain of all grace (Col. 2:9-10). Outside of Christ, there is no grace. Also, it can be said, 'Grace is poured *from* thy lips' (Heb. 1:1-2). When Christ, the Word of God, opens his lips as our surety, prophet, priest and king, grace is poured into our souls — living, saving, abundant grace. One word from him turned Saul of Tarsus into an apostle, a harlot into a repentant believer and a publican into a prince. **'Therefore God hath blessed thee for ever.'** Calvin renders it, *'Because* God hath blessed thee'. It is true that God has blessed our Mediator as a reward for his love and labour, and he deserves the recompense, but the great reason for his beauty, his grace and his salvation is that he is blessed for ever of the Father, who put all things in him (John 3:35; Eph. 1:3; 1 Cor. 1:30).

vv.3-4. What is **'thy sword'**? It is his word (Heb. 4:12; Eph. 6:17).
By his word the worlds were created and are governed. By his word
sinners are slain and conquered. By his word his enemies are
defeated. **'O most mighty, with thy glory and thy majesty.'** He
is almighty and so is able to make good all that he speaks, and to
make his word of precept, promise and condemnation effectual in
all that it is sent to do (Isa. 46:10-11; Num. 23:19). The holy war
in which he is engaged is the cause of **'truth and meekness and
righteousness'** and his gospel (his sword) will turn our error to
truth, our pride to meekness and our sinfulness to his righteousness! Are these not **'terrible'**, or, to use a better word, tremendous,
'things'? (Ps. 65:1-5).

v.5. **'Thine arrows are sharp.'** Our Lord uses no blunted sword or
pointless darts. His word is always effectual and can strike those
near or far with equal success. He aims for the hearts of his enemies,
not just their heads, so they are brought to fall at his feet in worship
and love (Rom. 5:10; Eph. 2:16; Col. 1:21). The arrows of his
judicial wrath are sharp, but the arrows of subduing grace are the
sharpest of all (John 6:37; 10:16).

vv.6-7.   The apostle Paul chose these words to identify and magnify our great prophet and priest. To the Son, Jesus Christ, the Father
says, **'Thy throne, O God, is for ever.'** Christ is God (John 1:1;
10:30; Acts 20:28). The reason why his throne is for ever and the
sceptre of his kingdom is righteousness, justice and truth is because
he is God.
       'Thou lovest righteousness.' He showed this in casting Adam
out from the garden, in all his dealings with Israel and the Old
Testament people and in working out a perfect righteousness for his
people (Rom. 3:19-26) and he will show it at the last day in wrath.
Because of who Christ is and what he has done, he is anointed above
all (Col. 1:14-18; Phil. 2:9-11).

v.8. **'Thy garments'** are Christ's offices, his honours, his righteousness. He is clothed with righteousness, honour and majesty
(Isa. 59:17; Ps. 104:1) and his garments smell, not of blood and
battle, but of sweet perfume 'in them that are saved', but that holy
odour is offensive to those who perish (2 Cor. 2:14-16).

The **'ivory palaces'** are his heavenly abode, where he is made glad in the presence of the Father and by the faith of his saints (Isa. 53:11; Luke 15:7).

vv.9-12. The church of the Lord Jesus shares his honour and happiness. He sets her in the place of dignity **'upon thy right hand'** and clothes her with the best, the priceless and the beautiful. Though some may have been paupers or princesses, yet all are in his bride at his right hand. They forget their own people and houses and look not back to Sodom or Jerusalem because he is their Lord and they worship him. The bride's beauty is her Lord's comeliness (Ezek. 16:11-14).

vv.13-15

1. The bride's new name is **'the king's daughter'**, because she is born of God and she is espoused to the Son of God.

2. The bride's character is **'all glorious within'** because of Christ who dwells in her.

3. The bride's **'clothing'** and **'raiment'** are wrought of gold of holiness and the needlework of his perfect righteousness, his atoning death and perfect obedience.

4. The bride's **'companions'** are all the redeemed of all ages.

5. The bride's entrance into her new home is being brought **'into the king's palace'** (John 14:1-3).

6. The bride's reception will be **'with gladness and rejoicing'**, no secret entrance but a triumphant and joyful acclaim (Ps. 24:7-10).

vv.16-17. The ancient fathers, such as Moses, Abraham and Isaac, are all gone, but their children and grandchildren are made kings and priests. And the name of Christ is remembered, exalted and magnified in all generations and among all nations. **'Therefore shall the people praise thee for ever and ever.'**

Let him be crowned with majesty
Who bowed his head in death,
And be his honours sounded forth
By all things that have breath.

10. The sinner's prayer

Psalm 51

William Plumer said, 'This psalm is fitly called the sinner's guide.' Luther said, 'No other psalm is oftener sung nor prayed in the church.' Thomas Chalmers said, 'This is the most deeply affecting of all the psalms, and I am sure the one most applicable to me.'

There are many ways to consider the psalm, but since it is the sinner's prayer, let us look at ten pleas or petitions made in this prayer.

1. **'Have mercy upon me, O God'** (v.1). Even before David mentions his sins, he appeals to the mercy of God. We do not deserve to be pardoned or forgiven; we deserve to be damned, so David does not ask for justice, but mercy. Pardon of sin must ever be an act of sovereign mercy (Exod. 33:18-19). Mercy is born of God's lovingkindness (1 John 4:10). Grace is God giving us what we *do not* deserve, and mercy is God *not* giving us what we *do* deserve.

2. **'According unto the multitude of thy tender mercies blot out my transgressions'** (v.1), the multitude of our transgressions from the womb to the grave. But here is comfort — our God is plenteous in redemption and has multitudes of mercies. David pleads guilty to many sins but asks that the record be obliterated, erased, blotted out, so that nothing remains. He desires not only pardon, but that there shall not be any remembrance of sin for ever (Isa. 43:25; 44:21-22; Heb. 10:17).

3. **'Wash me throughly from mine iniquity, and cleanse me from my sin'** (v.2). Sin defiles soul and body, makes us foul and filthy, separates us from God and corrupts even our good works (Isa. 64:6). Laws, works and legal washings will not help; God himself must wash us in his own blood (Acts 20:28). David pleads to be washed

and cleansed. Richard Baker says, 'Washing has to do with the work a-doing, and cleansing with the work done. Washing is done by the Lord; cleansing is the result.' Most people are concerned about the punishment of sin; David is concerned about the guilt of it. In verse 4 David acknowledges that his sins are against God, justifies God in condemning him and clears the name of God of any injustice when he is judged. This is true conviction and repentance.

4. **'Make me to know wisdom'** (v.6). True wisdom and under-standing of the righteousness of God, the nature of sin and the necessity of regeneration and the new birth are essential to faith, forgiveness and salvation.

Our sins are against God and he must be just and punish sin. He is 'a just God and a Saviour' (Isa. 45:21-22). Christ's life and death in our stead enable God to be both just and justifier (Rom. 3:25-26).

We were born in sin (v.5); sin is our nature. Our hearts are deceitful and desperately wicked; therefore, only the Spirit of God can teach us this truth and bring us to own it by giving us life and a new heart (vv.6,10). The wisdom of God in the inward part is Christ, who is made unto us wisdom (1 Cor. 1:30; John 6:44-45). We see the wisdom and power of God in the cross of substitution (1 Cor. 1:23-24).

5. **'Purge me with hyssop'** (v.7). This is what the publican prayed: 'Let thy blood be propitiation for me on the mercy-seat.' Let the sin-offering purge my sin and I shall be whiter than the snow (Heb. 10:11-14). All blood sacrifices sprinkled and offered in the Old Testament point to Christ, the Lamb of God (Heb. 1:3). Here is faith in Christ's atonement, its power and efficacy.

6. **'Make me to hear joy and gladness'** (vv.8-9). There is no greater misery than the guilt and fear of sin before God, and there is no greater joy than the joy of forgiveness and acceptance in Christ. He says, 'Lord, you speak peace, joy and gladness to my heart,' for faith, assurance and joy spring only from God. 'Set the bones which you have broken in revealing my iniquities, by blotting them out and being reconciled to me. Then I shall know joy and gladness.'

7. **'Create in me a clean heart, O God; and renew a right spirit within me'** (v.10). Sin has so destroyed us that the Creator must

come and, out of the death, darkness and ashes create a new heart, a new nature and a right spirit (Eph. 2:10; 2 Cor. 5:17; Gal. 6:15). David did not pray, 'Make my old heart clean'; he was too experienced in the helplessness and hopelessness of the old nature (Jer. 13:23). None but God can create a new heart or a new earth. 'Salvation is of the Lord' (Jonah 2:9). What a complete prayer in two sentences! 'Create' what was not there and 'renew' what is there but is in constant need of renewing.

8. **'Cast me not away from thy presence'** (v.11). 'Do not throw me away as unprofitable and worthless; banish me not from thy presence like Cain. Do not give me over to a reprobate mind' (Rom. 1:24-28).

'Take not thy Holy Spirit from me.' 'Thy Spirit is the spirit of life, light and truth. Permit me to be among those who share thy love, if only I keep the door' (Ps. 84:10). 'Lord, if you will, you can make me whole' (Matt. 8:1-2).

9. **'Restore unto me the joy of thy salvation'** (v.12). This sinner had known the joy of the Lord, but through sin he had lost that joy and longed for its return. Joy always follows pardon; it is presumption to think otherwise. None but God can forgive, give joy or restore it. 'Then I will teach others thy ways' (v.13). Huntington said, 'The degree S.S., or sinner saved, is more needful to teach others than an M.A. or a D.D.' A man cannot tell what he does not know any more than he can come back from where he has not been.

10. **'Deliver me from bloodguiltiness, O God'** (v.14). He had been the means of the death of Uriah, a faithful friend. Honest penitents do not cover their sins, but own them before God as they are. David's sins, whatever they were, are no more heinous than ours, committed in the heart. 'Open my lips to show forth thy praise. The formality of sacrifices and burnt offerings does not please thee' (v.16).

'The sacrifices of God are a broken spirit ... and a contrite heart,' because of sin, and a heart of faith in Christ Jesus, the Lamb of God who takes away our sins (Acts 20:20-21). Can you pray 'the sinner's prayer', which may be, as some say, 'Lord, be merciful to me, the sinner,' but contains all that David has set forth in this psalm? (Rom. 10:13).

11. 'My rock and my salvation'

Psalm 62

If, by the grace of God, I can learn a twofold lesson, my attitude will so totally change that I can never be the same again. That lesson is found in verse 1 of this psalm: **'My soul waiteth upon God'** and **'From him cometh my salvation.'**

1. *What* do I do? I wait as a disciple on my Lord's command. I wait as a bond-slave at my Master's feet. I wait as clay, submissive and surrendered in the Potter's hand (Rom. 9:20-23).

2. On *whom* do I wait? I wait on the sovereign, all-wise Lord, who works all things after the counsel of his own will (Eph. 1:9-12), on my heavenly Father, who loves me and works all things together for my good (Rom. 8:28).

3. *How* do I wait? I wait **'truly'**, or sincerely and silently. I wait only upon him. Note the repeated use of the word **'only'** in verses 2, 5 and 6.

4. *What are the results* of my seeking, looking and waiting upon God? 'From him cometh my salvation,' from the law's curse, from the judgement of sin, from the sting of death and from all condemnation (Rom. 8:1).

vv.2,6. **'He only is my rock and my salvation.'** This is the sum and substance of the Bible. I can find in Scripture no other doctrine than 'Salvation is of the Lord.' 'The salvation of the righteous is of the Lord' (Jonah 2:9; Ps. 3:8; 37:39; 2 Thess. 2:13). Moses exhorted the people to 'stand still [wait], and see the salvation of the Lord' (Exod. 14:13). It pleased the Lord to make us his people (1 Sam. 12:22); it pleased the Lord to bruise Christ in our stead (Isa. 53:10); it pleased the Lord to reveal Christ in us (Gal. 1:15); it pleased the Lord by the gospel to save those who believe (1 Cor. 1:21). He *only* is our rock and refuge! That 'rock' (typically and literally) is Christ (1 Cor. 10:4; Isa. 28:16). Christ is our defence against all charges and condemnation (Rom. 8:33-34), for he of God is made unto us all we need (1 Cor. 1:30).

'I shall not be greatly moved' — moved maybe, but not removed! We are like anchored ships that often swing with the tides and winds but are never swept away, because we are anchored on the rock, Christ Jesus (Heb. 6:19-20).

vv.3-4. The believer is never without enemies (Eph. 6:11-13; 1 Peter 5:8-9). It will be well to remember this. But, like David, it is best to begin with God, our rock and defence, and then to confront the enemy. Make sure of your relationship with the Lord before dealing with the enemy. The believer's enemies are real, but they are defeated and marked for destruction, as a bowing wall and a tottering fence which will collapse in due time.

What is *the goal* of the enemy? To bring the believer **'down from his excellency'**, which is his standing in Christ — his love for, dependence upon and total rest in Christ Jesus (Eph. 1:3-6; 2:4-9). This is the error of Rome, the error of Arminianism and the error of the modern cults, to mix works with grace, man's merits with the perfect righteousness of Christ and to preach salvation conditional on the will and works of man rather than on the will and work of our Lord (John 1:12-13; Rom. 9:15-16; Titus 3:5-6).

What are *the weapons* of the enemy? **'They delight in lies.'** They say, 'God has done all that he can do and now it is up to you. Take the first step and God will meet you. God helps those who help themselves.' Flattery and sentiment fall from their lips. They pretend to bless, while they totally destroy a man's hope for life. They cry, 'Peace, peace, when there is no peace.'

vv.5-8. Amid all these trials, conflicts and attacks from the enemies of his soul, the psalmist returns to his original hope as the dove returned to the ark. **'My soul, wait thou only upon God.'** The battle is his, and he only can justify me. **'My expectation is from him.'** In him dwell all fulness and all blessings; he will exalt me in due time (Ps. 27:14). **'He only is my rock and my salvation.'** My righteousnesses are filthy rags (Isa. 64:6). **'He only is my defence.'** If God be for me, who can be against me? (Rom. 8:31-32). What does it matter who is against me? I am complete in him. **'Trust in**

him at all times.' In times of prosperity or poverty I know how to abound and to be abased (Phil. 4:12-13). In times of fellowship or loneliness he will never leave me. In times of health, sickness or death he is my refuge. I will **'pour out [my] heart before him'**. His heart is set upon us; let us set our hearts on him. Turn your vessel upside down and let your inmost desires, thoughts, sorrows and joys be poured out like water before the Lord. Hide nothing from him, because nothing can be hid from him. We shall learn to pray when we learn to be open and honest before our Lord.

v.9.   Men of low degree and men of high degree are alike; they are all vanity and lies! The masses and majority are not to be trusted or followed. The élite, educated and intelligent only promise what they cannot produce and condemn what they do not understand. Wretched is the man who puts his trust in either the multitude or the leaders. They are all lighter than vanity. Have no confidence in the flesh (Phil. 3:3).

v.10.   Trust not in oppression, poverty or persecution. A man is not a child of God because he is poor and in need, nor is he a Christian because he has to work hard and eke out a living for his family the hard way. If your riches increase and life becomes easy, do not mistake this prosperity for the favour of God; it may be Satan's way of putting you at ease. Set not your heart upon worldly gain, for many evils are there — idolatry, covetousness, forgetfulness of God and neglect of worship (Jer. 9:23-24).

vv.11-12. 'God needs to speak only once, but I have heard this twice (with my ear and with my heart, in the letter and in the spirit) that power, salvation and spiritual blessings come only from God in Christ. Also unto our God belongs mercy (Ps. 130:7), and he will render to every man what that man deserves.' Those out of Christ shall be judged according to their works. Those in Christ shall be judged according to his works, which are theirs by imputation (Rom. 4:21-25).

12. Our Lord's sufferings for our sins

Psalm 69

C. H. Spurgeon said, 'This is a Psalm of David, but if any enquire of whom speaketh the Psalmist this? Of himself or some other man? I would reply, of himself *and* some other man — the Lord Jesus Christ.' This is indeed a Messianic psalm! No portion of the Old Testament Scriptures is more often quoted in the New Testament, with the exception of Psalm 22.

v.1. **'Save me, O God.'** His enemies mocked him, crying, 'He saved others; himself he cannot save' (Matt. 27:42). As our substitute, bearing our sins, he could not save himself, but rather offered up himself (Heb. 7:27; 9:14); and he was heard (Heb. 5:7-9).

'The waters are come in unto my soul.' Our Lord's chief sufferings were his soul agony (Isa. 53:9-10).

v.2. Our Lord calls his state under our sins **'deep mire'** and **'deep waters'**. Sin is as mire (Jer. 38:6) for its filthiness and its hold on men. In deep water there is no place to stand and the waters go over the head. The judgement of God is described as waters that overflow (Isa. 28:17). Our Lord is not a faint-hearted weakling; his sufferings were real and terrible.

v.3. He wept as a man of sorrows, acquainted with grief. He prayed until he sweated great drops of blood. His throat was dry and parched under the fires of God's wrath against our sins and he cried, 'I thirst.' He looked and waited for his God; but he was left alone, crying, 'My God, why hast thou forsaken me?'

v.4. 'They hated me without a cause' (John 15:25). From the cradle to the cross his enemies were without number. They were very many and very mighty. All earth and all hell despised him (Isa. 53:3; Acts

4:27), all without cause, for there was no sin or fault in him. **'I restored that which I took not away.'** Though innocent, he was treated as guilty. The sheep went astray, but the shepherd was smitten and on their behalf he restored the honour of God's justice and law and their happiness (Rom. 5:19; 1 Cor. 15:21-22; Ps. 23:3).

v.5. David might truly say this, but not our Lord, unless he refers to our sins imputed and laid to his charge. He was made to be sin for us (2 Cor. 5:21).

v.6. It seems to some that he prays that true believers will not be ashamed, confounded and confused by his crucifixion and death, but it may be better understood, 'Because I, for *their* sakes, do bear their shame, let them, for *my* sake, never be ashamed nor confounded' (1 Peter 2:6; Rom. 9:33).

vv.7-8. Christ died for our sake, to redeem us to God, but he was set forth to be a mercy-seat, to declare God's righteousness and to enable God to be both just and justifier (Rom. 3:25-26). Even his brothers did not believe him (John 7:5).

vv.9-10. Some men are eaten up with pride, covetousness and hatred, but the master-passion of Christ was his Father's glory, will and truth (John 2:13-17). The hatred of men for God fell upon Christ, and everything he did or said only increased their reproach.

vv.11-12. His being identified with us in our poverty, laying aside his eternal glory and clothing himself in flesh, humbling himself and being found in fashion as a man, should have won him acclaim and pity; but it only increased their mockings and revilings (Matt. 27:27-30). From the judges and leaders who sat in the gate to the drunkards on the street, all men by nature hated the living God (1 Cor. 2:14; Rom. 8:7).

vv.13-18. While they mocked and scoffed, our Lord prayed to the Father. Here in these verses is his prayer for victory and deliverance 'according to the multitude of thy tender mercies, according to thy lovingkindness, and according to the truth and promises of thy salvation'. He speaks as our representative, and as such his deliverance and redemption are ours.

v.19. Here are three words that describe our Lord's sufferings for us and the contempt poured upon him because of our sins — **'reproach ... shame, and ... dishonour'**. We deserve all three, but he bore them in our place (Isa. 53:4-6).

vv.20-21. Our Lord died with a broken heart (John 19:34-35). Reproach, loneliness and heaviness broke his heart. There is no suffering quite like it. In his thirst they gave him gall and vinegar (Matt. 27:34,48). Someone wrote,

> Whatever he sought for, there was none;
> Our Captain fought the field alone.
> As soon as the Chief to battle led,
> That moment every soldier fled.

vv.22-28. The Lord calls for judgement upon rebels and a judicial curse upon the despisers of the Lord's Christ. Their ceremonies, tables and types, which should reveal his redemptive work, only serve as a stumbling-block and a trap (Rom. 11:9-10). A veil is upon their eyes (2 Cor. 3:15). They persecute him whom the Lord hath smitten (Isa. 53:4,10). Iniquity is added to their iniquity; for they are now guilty of the blood of his Son and they are blotted out of the book of God (Exod. 32:33).

vv.29-30. Our Lord returns to prayer and praise. 'I am poor now, but shall be exalted' (Phil. 2:8-11). 'Even in the depths of agony I will praise and magnify him.'

vv.31-32. God never found pleasure or satisfaction in the sacrifices of the Old Testament, but he is fully pleased and reconciled through Christ's sufferings (Heb. 10:5-7). Those who are taught of God rejoice in him, and they live who seek God in Christ.

vv.33-35. Believers, in their own eyes, are poor and needy prisoners; but because of our Lord's redemptive work, they are in God's sight sons of God, complete in Christ (Col. 2:9-10). He will hear, despise not, save and build them on that rock.

v.36. They are the seed of Abraham (Gal. 3:29). They are heirs of God (Rom. 8:17). They love his name (1 John 5:1-2). They dwell in God (1 John 4:15).

13. 'Mercy and truth are met together'

Psalm 85

Our Lord told the disciples, 'All things must be fulfilled, which were written in the law of Moses, and in the prophets, and in the psalms, concerning me' (Luke 24:44). In preparing these studies on pictures of Christ in the Old Testament, it would be impossible to omit this psalm, if only for verse 10. God's mercy and truth, righteousness and peace meet *only* in Christ.

v.1. The author of this psalm speaks of the past mercy and favour of God to the land of Israel and the people of Israel. The Lord brought them out of bondage and captivity. But all believers are the true sons of Jacob and seed of Abraham (Rom. 2:28-29; Gal. 3:7,28-29). The land of the Lord is the kingdom of Christ, the church of Christ is true Israel and the true sons of Jacob (Mal. 3:6), and the captivity out of which he has brought us is the bondage of sin (Gal. 3:10,13). This is a psalm of victory and the rejoicing of all believers of all ages and nations.

vv.2-3. In these verses four things stand out prominently.

1. *The author of all spiritual blessings.* **'Thou hast...'**; *'Thou* **hast been favourable'**; *'Thou* **hast brought back the captivity...'**; *'Thou* **hast forgiven...'**; *'Thou* **hast covered...'**; *'Thou* **hast taken away...'** Salvation is of the Lord in its entirety, from its origination in eternity past to its future consummation in glory (Rom. 8:29-30).

2. *The people who are so blessed are his people.* 'Jacob have I loved; Esau have I hated' (Rom. 9:11-16). They are his people by divine choice (John 6:37-39), his people by divine purchase (Acts 20:28; John 10:11) and his people by a divine call (1 Cor. 1:26-30).

3. *The blessing of his covenant.* **'Thou hast forgiven the iniquity of thy people'** — not without price, for he was bruised for our iniquities (Isa. 53:4-6) and our iniquity was laid on him. The reference here is to the scapegoat of Leviticus 16:20-22.

'Thou hast covered all their sin.' God set forth Christ to be a mercy-seat and a covering for sin, as the blood was sprinkled upon the mercy-seat of old (Lev. 16:15-16; Rom. 3:25).

4. *The extent of these blessings.* **'Thou hast forgiven … *all* their sin'** (1 John 1:7; Heb. 10:17) and **'Thou hast taken away *all* thy wrath'** (Rom. 5:1; 8:1).

vv.4-5. In salvation there is the removal of God's wrath upon us (2 Cor. 5:19), and there is the removal of our enmity towards him. 'Be ye reconciled to God' (2 Cor. 5:20). Both are accomplished by the power of God (Ps. 110:3). The wrath of God is turned from us by the obedience and death of Christ, and our enmity is turned away in regeneration by the Holy Spirit giving us a new heart to love God (Rom. 5:5).

v.6. When we were dead men, like Ezekiel's bones, God revived us and give us life in Christ. **'Wilt thou not revive us again?'** And again? For we are in constant need of refreshing and renewal by his Spirit.

'That thy people may rejoice in thee' — never in themselves or their own doings (Phil. 3:3). We can find at all times ten thousand reasons to rejoice in the Lord and in his mercy.

v.7. **'Show us thy mercy, O Lord'.** It is the of Lord's mercies that we are not consumed (Lam. 3:22-26); all is mercy from first to last. Mercy passed by us in our blood and said, 'Live'. Mercy covered our nakedness with his robe of righteousness. Mercy washed away our sins and gave us repentance and faith. Mercy keeps us in the way and will not let us go until mercy has wrought its perfect work, conforming us to his image.

'Grant us thy salvation.' It is 'thy salvation'. The plan is his, the provision is his, the application is his, the sustaining power is his and the consummation is his. It is all of grace! The work whereby a dead, defiled sinner is lifted from the dunghill, washed and made ready for the presence of the Lord is of God and of him only. Lord, grant to us that perfect salvation!

v.8. 'I will hear thy Word, O Lord!' Oh, how vital is the Word of God to his people! By his Word he speaks peace in Christ. His Word is the foundation of faith (Rom. 10:17), the source of comfort, the means of growth (1 Peter 2:2) and the children's bread. Let us not turn again to sin nor to the beggarly elements, but find rest and all we need in him. There is no provision, protection against sin and apostasy, nor daily peace to be found anywhere except in his Word!

v.9. Our Lord is always near and with them that fear him, no matter the circumstances. He will never leave nor forsake us (Phil. 1:6), that he may be glorified and his glory may dwell in his kingdom.

v.10. **'Mercy and truth are met together; righteousness and peace have kissed each other.'** Oh, what a declaration! What good news! These four divine attributes parted, as far as we are concerned, at the fall of Adam. Mercy was inclined to save man and peace could not be his enemy; but truth must order the death of the rebel, for 'God will by no means clear the guilty', and righteousness demands perfect obedience to every jot and tittle of God's holy law. All of the divine attributes are in Christ, for he is very God of very God, but mercy and truth met in Christ on our behalf, and righteousness and peace kissed each other at Calvary. God is a just God *and* a Saviour! In the obedience and death of Christ for sinners, God is enabled to be both just and justifier (Rom. 3:25-26).

v.11. Promises which lie unfulfilled like buried seeds will spring up in full view (Heb. 11:13) and God's righteousness will rest upon his people like an open window in heaven. The person of Christ explains this verse most sweetly. In him **'truth'** is found in our humanity (Isa. 53:1) and his deity brings **'righteousness'** to us from heaven (2 Cor. 5:21).

vv.12-13. Every good and perfect gift is from him and nothing good will he withhold from his people. He has willed our eternal good and is working all things together to accomplish it (Rom. 8:28). The righteousness by which we are justified and accepted in Christ has gone before and he has set us in the steps our Lord already walked.

14. The victory of the Messiah

Psalm 91

Many believe this psalm was written by Moses, because the psalm preceding it is credited to him. Others believe that David is the author and the person spoken of is Solomon, his son. But this psalm certainly speaks of the Messiah and contains promises of protection and safety to him, as man, from diseases, evil spirits and wicked men, under the care of angels. Satan referred to this psalm on the mount of temptation (Matt. 4:6). This is truly the victory of the Messiah and of everyone that is in him, represented by him and perfected by him. Every believer is always under divine care and protection (1 Peter 5:7; Ps. 37:5; Heb. 1:14).

1. The believer's dwelling-place

vv.1-2. **'The secret place of the most High'** is within the veil (Heb. 6:19-20) in the very presence of God, seated with Christ (Eph. 2:5-6). By the righteousness and blood of Christ we not only come into God's presence, but we dwell there, never to leave (Heb. 10:19-22). We **'abide under the shadow'** or protection of the almighty God, like small chicks under the wings of the mother hen (Ps. 17:8-9). No harm can come to us, because the Lord is our **'refuge and ... fortress'**. Even the gates of hell shall not prevail (Matt. 16:18; John 10:27-29; Rom. 8:35-39). Our assurance and confidence are only in him, as he is described by four names

We come reverently only through the blood of Christ for he is **'the most High'** and is holy.

We rest in him because he is **'the Almighty'** and is sovereign.

We rejoice in his salvation because he is **'the Lord'**, Jehovah.

We trust in him as **'my God'**; everything is here because he is our God (Col. 2:9-10).

2. *The believer's confidence*

vv. 3-8. Someone said, 'I love the "shalls" and "wills" of God's Word.' There is no 'maybe', 'perhaps', or uncertainty connected with the purpose and promises of God in Christ Jesus (Ps. 23:6; John 10:16).

The Lord Jesus shall **'deliver'** us from the curse of the law (Gal. 3:13), from the penalty of sin (Rom. 8:1), from the wrath of God (Rom. 8:33-34) and from all enemies, even invisible enemies (Eph. 6:12).

The Lord Jesus shall **'cover'** us with his spotless robe of righteousness, his glorious wedding garment (2 Cor. 5:3). His **'wings'** are both for healing and hiding, and his **'truth'** (his word of promise and faithfulness) will turn to flight every enemy (Luke 4:1-13).

Because Christ is our Redeemer, we shall not fear the terrors of the night — neither men nor devils; we shall not fear the arrows of the day — wars, floods, accidents, or earthquakes; we shall not fear the **'pestilence that walketh in darkness'** — diseases, plagues and demons; we shall not fear the **'destruction that wasteth at noon-day'** — the final judgement of God upon the earth. He has hedged about his children (Job 1:10), and neither devils, men, nor death can touch one without his permission.

Evil may be near the child of God, but not upon him. The plague that killed the firstborn in Egypt was near the Israelites, but it did not strike them. God's people will have trials, tribulations and infirmities in the flesh, but only by the will of the Father. They will die, but only when he decrees, never as the result of any other will or reason. With our eyes we shall see the judgements of God upon an evil race and shall agree with his judgements and praise him for our deliverance.

3. *The believer's Redeemer and refuge*

vv.9-13. Here is the only reason that we dwell within the veil, that we are delivered from all condemnation and judgement, that we are covered with his righteousness, hidden under his protective wings and have no fear of terror here or hereafter: because the Lord is our refuge and our dwelling-place. There is no safety or security anywhere, nor in anyone, but Christ Jesus — not in religion, law, works, or morality — only in Christ (Gal. 2:21; 3:11-13; Acts 13:38-39; Rom. 5:1-2). It is true that **'Thou hast made the Lord ... thy habitation,'** willingly and sincerely; but we love him because he loved us; we come to him because he came to us; we have made him our Lord and refuge because he made us his people and called us to faith (John 15:16; 1:12-13; Rom. 9:15-16). To God be the glory!

The angels (created spirits, who are made by the Lord and at his command) are ministering spirits to his people. They encamp about them and are committed to their care by him who is Lord of heaven and earth.

4. The believer's promises

vv.14-16. Here is the Lord God himself speaking of his chosen ones.

'Because he hath set his love upon me' — not because they deserve mercy, but with all their imperfections they do love the Lord (John 21:17). There is first his love for us without our love; then there is our love for his love, which is genuine and sincere.

'Therefore' — there is always a 'because' and a 'therefore' in law and grace. Because we sinned, therefore we die! Because Christ died, therefore we live! Because we believe and love Christ, therefore:

> **'[I will] deliver him'** from sin, Satan and wrath.
> **'I will set him on high'** in Christ.
> **'I will answer him'**, when he prays and when he seeks mercy.
> **'I will be with him in trouble'** (Rom. 8:28).
> **'I will honour him'** (John 12:26).
> **'With long life will I satisfy him'**, not here necessarily, but with eternal life;
> **'[I will] show him my salvation'** (Exod. 33:18-19; 2 Cor. 4:6).

15. 'Bless the Lord, O my soul'

Psalm 103

A few things are worthy of notice at the beginning of our study.

1. Most agree that this is a psalm of David's latter years, for there is a clear sense of the frailty of this life; there is a keener awareness of sin; and there is a high priority placed on mercy and forgiveness.

2. Not one petition or request occurs throughout the entire psalm. This is another sign of spiritual maturity — more praise and less petition, more gratitude and less 'give me'. As we grow in grace, our prayers change.

3. The name Jehovah is mentioned eleven times in twenty-two verses. The psalmist kneels in adoration and praises the Lord himself. It is possible to be taken up with blessings, gifts and benefits and fail to praise the Lord himself!

vv.1-2. **'Bless the Lord, O my soul.'** This is the highest form of praise. Not just the lips, but my heart, my innermost being, my soul, loves and praises the Lord. Blessed is the man who has learned to converse with himself concerning spiritual truth (Ps. 4:4; 77:6).

'All that is within me, bless his holy name.' Let my judgement bless him by submitting to his Word. Let my imagination bless him by holy meditation. Let my affections bless him by loving what he loves. Let my desires bless him by seeking his will. Let my hope bless him by restful assurance and peace. 'Bless his holy name.' His name signifies his nature and attributes. I bless and rejoice in him as he is revealed in his Word written and in his Word incarnate. 'Let God be God!' The holiness of God is his chief attribute and glory. The holiness of his name is that which beautifies all that he is and does. He is a just God and a Saviour (Isa. 45:21). He is righteous and merciful (Ps. 85:10; Rom. 3:26).

The psalmist's praise and gratitude has four attributes:

1. It is personal — **'my soul'**.
2. It is sincere — **'all that is within me'**.
3. It is constant — **'forget not'**.
4. It is specific — **'all his benefits'**. My all praises his all!

vv.3-5. David begins a list of his benefits.

'Who forgiveth all thine iniquities.' Forgiveness is of God, who delights to show mercy. It is from God, who only can forgive. It is in Christ, who is our ransom, redemption and righteousness. And it is complete with God, who forgives all our iniquities (Eph. 1:7; 1 John 1:7).

'Who healeth all thy diseases.' The diseases of this body are the results of sin and God will heal them when it is according to his will and when it serves his purpose, but the diseases referred to here are spiritual diseases which, like our sins, are all healed in Christ. He bore *all* our spiritual sicknesses and diseases in his body on the tree and by his sufferings we are healed for ever (Isa. 53:4-5; Matt. 8:17).

'Who redeemeth thy life from destruction.' We must die — all men do; we may die violently or in great pain — many have done so; but we shall never perish! Christ, our righteousness, redeems us from the curse of the law (Gal. 3:13). Christ, our sin-offering, has redeemed us from the judgement of sin (Rom. 8:1,33-34). Christ, our risen Lord, has redeemed us from the grave (John 11:25-26).

'Who crowneth thee with lovingkindness and tender mercies.' Earthly kings are crowned with material crowns of gold, silver and diamonds, symbols of their material kingdoms which will all pass away. We are kings and priests, crowned, dignified and beautified with the love, mercy and grace of God, which is his kingdom of righteousness and peace and will never pass away. Our crowns are not of gold, but glory, and our robes are royal robes of his righteousness.

'Who satisfieth thy mouth with good things.' No natural man is ever satisfied or at peace, for the things of this world can never satisfy the soul. But the 'good things' of Christ (John 16:15; 3:35; Rom. 8:31,37; 1 Cor. 3:21) are ours, and all these good things satisfy our appetites and needs so that our **'youth is renewed'**. The youth and strength of grace are constantly renewed and while the outward man may decay, the inward man is renewed day by day until we are carried into his presence (2 Cor. 4:16; Ps. 17:15). God's people, even in old age, have a keen spiritual eye, an open ear to his Word and they run and are not weary (Isa. 40:31).

v.6. Going on from personal blessing to the general righteous justice and judgement of God, David declares that all injustice and oppression shall receive just retribution at the hand of God (Deut. 32:35; Rom. 12:19).

v.7. God made known unto Moses **'his ways'** of mercy and grace in Christ (John 5:46). He did not leave Moses to discover truth for himself. God alone can reveal himself (Luke 10:22; 1 Cor. 2:9-14). The people of Israel saw less than Moses, for they beheld the **'acts'** of God without understanding or seeing the glory of his grace in Christ.

vv.8-14. In these verses David rejoices in the Lord's feelings for, and dealings with, his chosen people in Christ. We are sinners and are always in need of his compassion and grace. His mercy forgives sin, his grace bestows favour, his long-suffering and patience give space for repentance and faith and his abundant compassion will never fail. Why has he not **'dealt with us after our sins'**? Is it not because he has dealt with Christ for our sins and iniquities? (1 Peter 3:18; 2:24). Our minds cannot comprehend his great mercy to us in Christ. It is higher than the heavens. Our sins are covered, blotted out and removed as far from us as the east is from the west — infinity! They are remembered no more. The guilt of sin can no more return than east can become west. 'Such pity and love as a father has to his children dear, like pity shows the Lord to all who worship him in fear.' Our Lord knows how and of what we are made, for he made us! He knows our weaknesses, infirmities and flesh. He knows we are made of dust, are dust still and will return to dust (Heb. 4:15).

vv.15-18. Men are like the grass and the flower, which live but for a season and are soon gone; but the mercy of the Lord in his covenant of grace in Christ Jesus is everlasting and his righteousness shall endure for ever upon those who believe (Rom. 8:16-23). For ever in glory with him is our inheritance!

vv.19-22. David closes with a grand chorus which springs from his knowledge of the boundless power and glorious sovereignty of God.

His throne is fixed in the heavens; his government is over all and knows no alarm, disorder, or surprises. He will accomplish his purpose and be glorified. Therefore, let everything that hath breath praise and bless the Lord — especially my soul!

16. 'Let the redeemed of the Lord say so'

Psalm 107

The theme of this psalm is thanksgiving and praise to the Lord for his goodness and his wonderful works of redemption and deliverance to the children of men (vv.1,8,15,21,31).

Men in general do not see or own the goodness of the Lord to sinful men, but the **'redeemed of the Lord'** rejoice in his mercy and they say so! (vv.1-2). They have actually experienced, under Holy Spirit conviction, all that is written in this psalm and rejoice in his special grace and mercy in delivering them (Ps. 103:1-5).

This psalm is a vivid picture of the sinner's bondage, his troubles and sorrows in sin, his inability to find a way out, his cry unto the Lord for mercy and God's sovereign mercy to the sinner in Christ. Each section ends with: **'He saved them out of their distresses.'**

The last verse reveals the importance of the psalm: **'Whoso is wise, and will observe these things, even they shall understand the lovingkindness of the Lord'** (v.43; 1 John 5:20).

v.1. **'The Lord ... is good.'** His goodness and mercy are especially magnified in the unworthiness of their objects. His mercy is both for ever and endures for ever. His mercy to us in Christ preceded our call and cry and will endure despite our failures. He is good when he takes away as well as when he gives, when he wounds and when he heals, when he frowns and when he smiles. 'The Lord ... is good', for there is none good but the Lord.

v.2. Particular redemption leads to special praise. Salvation is of the Lord from its origination to its consummation; and the 'redeemed of the Lord' acknowledge that they are what they are by the grace of God!

v.3. We were in bondage to the law, captives of sin, under the curse, condemnation and sentence of divine justice, and he, by his obedience and death, redeemed us (1 Peter 1:18-21). A full atonement has been made, the price is paid and there is no charge nor condemnation that can be laid against us (Rom. 8:31-34). He has gathered in Christ all whom he purposed to save and all whom he purchased by his blood from every nation under heaven (Rev. 5:9; Eph. 1:10-12).

vv.4-9. Here is our fall and the lost state of men by nature and our misery and inability to find any peace or rest. We are brought to a right sense of our condition and cry to the Lord Jesus for deliverance. He hears us and delivers us out of all our distresses.

We wander **'in the wilderness'**, lost in sin, lonely, for like sheep, we have gone astray to our own way (Isa. 53:6). We find no place to dwell, for there is none! God only is our dwelling-place.

'Hungry and thirsty.' This is Holy Spirit conviction, for God must make us willing in the day of his power (Ps. 110:3). Holy Spirit conviction of sin leads to spiritual hunger and thirst, which can only find satisfaction in Christ.

'Their soul fainted in them.' There is no one to help. Like the woman with the issue of blood, we can find no help on this earth.

'Then they cried unto the Lord in their trouble.' Not until a man really becomes lost, not until he thirsts for forgiveness and realizes that no one but God can deliver him from this lost, helpless condition, will he cry unto the Lord Jesus. Peter cried, 'Lord, save me or I perish.' The helpless leper cried, 'Lord, if you will, you can make me clean' (Matt. 8:1-3). The thief on the cross acknowledged his sin, his just condemnation and cried for mercy.

'He delivered them out of their distresses.' Do you see why they gave thanks? Do you see why they praise him? Do you see why they cry, 'Unto him who hath loved us and washed us from sin, unto him be the glory for ever, Amen'?

He delivered us out of our trouble and distresses and also, **'He led them forth by the right way.'** This is the way of righteousness in Christ Jesus (Ps. 23:3; 2 Cor. 5:21; Rom. 10:1-4). He has made us righteous, holy and umblameable, that we **'might go to a city of habitation'** — his presence, his glory, his heaven! Abraham looked for that city (Heb. 11:10).

'Oh that men would praise the Lord!' give him the glory, own and declare that the salvation of the righteous is of the Lord (2 Tim. 1:9; Titus 3:5-6).

'He satisfieth the longing soul, and filleth the hungry soul with goodness.' Our Lord saves us out of our sin and he gives us a righteousness which assures us of eternal glory, but he also, here and now, satisfies our souls with his presence, peace, rest and joy. His daily grace is sufficient and his presence a delight. Our ultimate satisfaction will be to awake in his likeness (Isa. 26:3-4; Phil. 4:6-7; Ps. 17:15).

vv.10-16,17-21,23-31. All these illustrations and pictures tell the story of God's sovereign grace to sinners in Christ. Holy Spirit conviction of sin leads to a realization of our state of misery and condemnation. In the light of God's holiness and God's Word, we see our inability and the impossibility of human help, which causes us to cry in our troubles unto him who 'is able to save to the uttermost' (Heb. 7:25). He is not only willing, but able, to save, for he has somewhat to offer (Heb. 8:1-3).

v.32. Those who know who he is, what he has done and where our great Lord is now will certainly exalt him, magnify his name and give him all glory in the congregation.

vv.33-41. God is the first cause of all things (1 Sam. 2:3-10; Job 1:21). Especially in redemption will God glorify his grace by humbling the proud and exalting the humble (James 4:6). 'He turns the rivers of the proud into a wilderness and the wilderness of the humble into standing water.'

v.42. The righteous know this and rejoice; all others shall stop their mouths.

17. The King-Priest

Psalm 110

No study of Christ in the Old Testament can ignore this psalm. Note how many times verses 1 and 4 are referred to in the New Testament (Matt. 22:44; Acts 2:34-35; Heb. 1:13; 5:6; 6:20; 7:17). The Old Testament reveals Jesus Christ in promise, picture and pattern, and in the New Testament Christ comes to earth in person (Matt. 1:21-23). This psalm is a clear revelation of the person and office of the Lord Jesus.

v.1. **'The Lord'** (the Father) **'said unto my Lord'** (the Son, Jesus Christ). Oh that we might understand just a little of the power of the Word of God! 'And God said...' — this is enough! All of the great works of grace are brought into being by the Word of God. Had he not spoken, there would be no manifestation of deity to us (John 1:1-4). When he speaks, nothing can change it. 'I have spoken it; I will bring it to pass' (Isa. 46:11).

David knew that the Lord our God is one God, yet he distinguishes between the Father and 'my Lord' — his Shepherd and Redeemer. Thomas uses the same term: 'My Lord and my God'. The Father sent the Son into the world as our Lord and Saviour (John 3:14-16; Gal. 4:4-5), yet 'I and my Father are one' (John 10:30).

'Sit thou at my right hand.' This is an oft-quoted passage because it declares that Jesus Christ has successfully finished what he undertook to accomplish on earth — the full and complete redemption of his people (John 17:4; Heb. 10:11-14). No earthly priest ever sat down in the tabernacle, for his work was never done! Christ sits as our representative and intercessor. He sits because all is safe and there is no cause for alarm. He sits at Jehovah's right hand because omnipotence waits to accomplish his will (John 6:37-39). Every enemy will be subdued and all the elect will come to him.

v.2. **'Zion'** is the church or true Israel. What, then, is that rod of his strength? It is the gospel, illustrated by Moses' rod. It was by his rod that Moses wrought wonders, smote the Egyptians, divided the sea and brought water from the rock. The Lord sends his gospel out of the church to call his elect. Salvation is the result of the preaching of the gospel (Mark 16:15-16; 2 Cor. 2:14-16). The Lord Jesus reigns over the willing and the unwilling (John 17:1-2), but his gospel of truth is the rod of strength that awakens dead sinners (Eph. 1:13; James 1:18; 1 Cor. 15:1-3).

v.3. **'Thy people shall be willing in the day of thy power'** (see 1 Thess. 1:4-5). The gospel is the power of God unto salvation (Rom. 1:16); and when the rod of his strength (the gospel) is preached in the power of his Spirit, his people willingly believe and embrace Christ.

1. The *promise* is made to Christ — **'thy people'**, which were given by the Father, purchased by his blood and called by the Spirit.
2. The *disposition* of his people — **'shall be willing'**. They are willing to turn from all idols; they are willing to forsake their own thoughts; they are willing to bow to Christ as Prophet, Priest and King; they are extremely willing to receive Christ and rest only in him to redeem them.
3. The *character* of his people — **'in the beauties of holiness'**. They are arrayed in the beautiful garment of Christ's righteousness and holiness.
4. The *number* of his people — they are as the dew **'from the womb of the morning'**.

v.4. 'Here is the heart of the psalm and the very centre and soul of our faith,' said C. H. Spurgeon. 'Our Lord Jesus is the Priest-King by the eternal oath of Jehovah.'

'The Lord hath sworn.' It must be the most solemn and sure matter which leads the eternal God to swear (Heb. 6:16-20) and to add, 'and will not change'. It is done and done for ever: Jesus Christ is the surety, priest-king and only mediator of his people (1 Tim. 2:5; John 14:6).

Aaron and his sons were types of Christ, but with limitations (Heb. 10:11-12). They were many; he one. They were men; he is the

God-man. They were only priests; he is king-priest. They died; he lives. Their priesthood had a beginning and an end; his is for ever. They offered many sacrifices; he offered one. They offered animal blood; he gave his own blood. They ministered in an earthly sanctuary; he in heaven. Their sacrifices could never take away sin; his perfected for ever!

Read of the appearance of Melchizedek in Genesis 14:17-20 and Hebrews 7:1-4. Melchizedek's office was exceptional; none preceded nor succeeded him. He comes upon the page of history mysteriously and goes away — no birth, no pedigree, no death — and he blessed Abraham. He is called the priest of the Most High God and the King of peace! He was seen only once, and that once was enough.

Our Lord was made a priest by the Father; no one was before him nor after him; his order begins and ends in himself. He came once into the world and left his blessings upon the believing seed, and now he sits in glory exercising that merit and power on our behalf (Heb. 10:12-14).

vv.5-7. These last three verses show the future victory and judgements of Christ over and upon his enemies. He will not sit for ever, but will descend from heaven and destroy the works of evil.

'The day of his wrath.' As there is a time of grace and patience, so there is an appointed day of wrath and vengeance of our God. The wicked will not go unpunished. 'Their foot shall slide in due time' (Deut. 32:35).

He **'shall strike through kings ... judge among the heathen** [or nations] ... **wound the heads'** of great countries. What are the kings of the earth when they oppose the King of kings? All nations shall yield to his power or be crushed before it. He shall wound the heads of nations, heads of movements and Satan's head. All who will not have Christ to be their head shall be destroyed (Rom. 10:9-10; Phil. 2:9-11).

Drinking from the brook in the way pictures a confident warrior who is sure of victory, a patient warrior who, without hurry, pursues the foe and a victorious warrior who lifts up his head triumphantly in an easy victory.

18. The chief cornerstone

Psalm 118:1-24

One reason why I have chosen for us to study this psalm is because of what Martin Luther said: 'This is my psalm, my chosen psalm. I love them all; I love all Holy Scripture, which is my consolation and my life. But this psalm is nearest to my heart and I have a particular right to call it my own. It has saved me from many a pressing danger. It is my friend, dearer to me than all the honours and powers of the earth. Would to God that all men would claim the psalm as especially theirs.'

Another reason is because of the number of times the New Testament refers to verse 22 (Matt. 21:42; Acts 4:11-12; Eph. 2:20). If the Lord Jesus and the apostles select an Old Testament scripture and apply it to our Redeemer, it would be wise for us to consider it in our study of Old Testament pictures of Christ. This psalm, indeed, belongs to the Messiah and though David is the author, we hear Christ, the son of David, speak.

v.1. **'O give thanks unto the Lord,'** for all his mercies, temporal and spiritual, in the name of Christ (Eph. 1:3).

'For he is good'; goodness is his nature and essence. He is the fountain of all goodness and the author of all good things (James 1:17).

'His mercy endureth for ever.' All of his goodness to us is mercy, for we are undeserving sinners. He told Moses that his chief glory is his goodness and his eternal mercies (Exod. 33:18-19; Rom. 9:15-16).

vv.2-4. **'Let Israel now say, that his mercy endureth for ever'** — not only those he led from Egypt, but all true Israel, both Jew and Gentile (Rom. 2:28-29). The Israel that God has chosen and redeemed in Christ rejoices in his eternal covenant mercies.

'Let the house of Aaron now say, that his mercy endureth for ever' — not just those priests who went into the Holy of Holies with the sacrifice, but all believers; for we are all priests of God and offer spiritual sacrifices unto him, especially praise (Heb. 10:19).

'Let them now that fear the Lord say, that his mercy endureth for ever.' A truly God-fearing man, conscious of his sin and need, is deeply conscious of God's mercy! 'There is forgiveness with thee, that thou mayest be feared' (Ps. 130:4).

v.5. The Lord heard David in his distress and exalted him to a large place, the throne of Israel. And so he did our Messiah when he raised him from the dead and exalted him to his own right hand. He has brought all believers out of the pit into large places, such as the liberty of Christ, green pastures, still waters and, ultimately, God's heaven. 'If the Son ... shall make you free, ye shall be free indeed' (John 8:36).

vv.6-7. 'The Lord is for me' (Rom. 8:31). Who can be against me? Man can do nothing more than God permits. Our Messiah had no fear of all the faces of evil against him on earth or in the universe. The Messiah shall reign until the last enemy, which is death, shall be destroyed (1 Cor. 15:25-26). No enemy shall succeed against his church (Rom. 8:35-39).

vv.8-9. It is good, wise and safe to trust only in the Lord. He is willing, able, faithful to his Word and unchanging in his promises. Man is none of these things (Phil. 3:3), not even princes nor the chief among them.

vv.10-12. All the neighbouring nations round about Judea were enemies of Israel. David fought against them and in the name and power of the Lord defeated them as he did Goliath. But these verses especially seem to refer to the Messiah (Acts 4:26-28; Isa. 53:1-3; Ps. 22:11-16). They are like bees in the number and wrath of them, or like thorns, which are useless and fit only to be burned, yet they cause great pain. But in the name of the Lord, in the majesty of his name, calling upon God to glorify him, for the accomplishment of his purpose, Christ shall defeat and destroy sin, Satan, the world, death and hell (Isa. 53:10-12).

vv.13-14. It being in the name and power of the Lord that his enemies were destroyed when they came upon him, David gives all the glory to God. **'The Lord helped me. The Lord is my strength and song, and … my salvation.'** Apply this to the Messiah. The Father raised him from the dead and seated him at his right hand (Acts 2:22-24; 13:28-30; Phil. 2:8-11).

vv.15-16. All Israel rejoiced when David was raised to the throne, as throughout the heavens and earth the voice of rejoicing is heard on account of the victory of Christ, our Lord (Ps. 24:7-10). **'The right hand of the Lord doeth valiantly'** and **'is exalted'**. Is this not Christ, who sits at God's right hand? (Ps. 110:1; Heb. 1:3).

vv.17-18. David knew that he must die physically, as all men die, but 'I shall dwell in the house of the Lord for ever' and **'declare the works of the Lord'**. Christ said, 'He that believeth on me shall never die.' Over such the second death has no power. Again this refers to the Messiah who was chastened severely for our sins (Isa. 53:4-6) but he saw no corruption and ever lives. He died but for ever lives, and because he lives, we shall live.

vv.19-21. Who but Christ can require **'the gates of righteousness'** to be opened to him? By his obedience and blood the gates of the holiest are opened to him and his people (Ps. 24:3-10). Our glorious Redeemer is our sanctification, righteousness and the author and finisher of our salvation. We are righteous in him (2 Cor. 5:21) and enter glory by him.

v.22. **'The stone which the builders refused is become the head stone of the corner.'** No doubt who this is! Read Matthew 21:42-44 and Acts 4:10-12. He is the tried stone, the precious cornerstone, the sure foundation (Isa. 28:16), which the Jews refused. He is the fulfilment of all that their tabernacle, types and sacrifices represented, but they could not see (Rom. 11:7-10) and would not see!

v.23. This stone is from the Lord God. Christ is of his appointment and his will, and the laying, and even the rejection of that cornerstone are through his permission and will (Acts 2:23; 4:27-28). His death, resurrection and exaltation are of the Lord and our understanding of, and faith in, him are the Lord's doings. He is precious, marvellous, and so is his grace!

v.24. This day of redemption, reigned over by the Sun of righteousness, is the day God has made from all eternity! Those who have eyes to see and hearts to believe rejoice and are glad in it (2 Cor. 6:2).

19. The observer and the observed

Psalm 139

There is nothing more dishonouring to God, nor a greater denial of the very character of God, than for us, in his name, to pretend to be what we are not, to use words that are not sincere and which do not come from the heart and to do works of religion for the admiration and applause of men (1 Sam. 16:7; Luke 16:15). The Lord Jehovah knows us, understands us and is intimately acquainted with our persons, nature and character. It is so important that we know the God who knows us! (John 17:3; 1 John 5:20; 2 Tim. 1:12). There is nothing in us that God does not know.

v.1. I am a very small part of this universe, yet the Lord knows me as thoroughly as if he had examined me minutely, as if he had searched me individually with his sovereign eye. This infallible knowledge has always existed, for he has searched me. It is 'Jehovah and me'. With him I have to do (Heb. 4:13).

vv.2-4.
1. He knows all my movements — **'my downsitting and ... uprising'**, whether I sit down to read, watch television, write, or rise up to walk, work or play.
2. He knows all my thoughts — what they have been, what they are now and what they will be.
3. He knows my actions. He encircles me, whether awake or asleep, and is acquainted with my ways, my motives and my purposes.
4. He knows my words. Indeed, there has never been a word on my tongue that is not registered in the mind of God. He knows these words **'altogether'** — the source of them, the reason for them and the results of them.

v.5. God not only beholds us, but he besets us. He surrounds us and hems us in. There is no escape, for he is before and behind us and lest anyone think that his surrounding presence is distant, he adds, **'and laid thine hand upon me'** (John 17:2) to deal in mercy or judgement (e.g. Pharaoh, Rom. 9:17; Paul, Acts 9:15).

v.6. The omnipotence, the omniscience and the omnipresence of God are **'too wonderful for me'** to understand. The wisdom, the glory, the holiness of God are too high for me. At my most enlightened height, his every attribute is higher than the heavens above me (Rom. 11:33-36).

　　1. The attributes of God make sure his promises, yet they are too high for me.
　　2. The incarnation of Christ is the most complete manifestation of God, yet unexplainable.
　　3. Redemption by the death of Christ is the highest guarantee of our salvation, but who can explain it?
　　4. The resurrection will satisfy the highest hope of sinners, but no one knows the mystery of it.
　　5. How do you account for his inspired Word? Or the power of his gospel? Oh, 'that I may know him and the power of his resurrection'! (Phil. 3:10).

vv.7-12. Notice how the psalmist makes this matter personal to himself. If aware of my sin, full of fear at the presence of the Most High God, desiring to escape that confrontation with his holiness, where shall I go? Where shall I flee? The highest, the deepest, the remotest are all his dwelling-places. Darkness and light are both alike to God!

v.13. 'God owns me! He not only observes me and knows me, but he is the owner and Lord of my innermost parts. Even when I was hidden in my mother's womb, he covered me. In my most secret parts (**"my reins"**) and in my most secret condition (not yet born), I am under the ownership and control of my God.'

vv.14-16. I would not be dogmatic here, but it appears that David turns from the observer to the observed, from marvelling at the mysteries of God to rejoicing in the mercies of God: **'I will praise thee.'**

1. **'I am fearfully and wonderfully made,'** and this is true of me in my fourfold state: created in Adam; fallen in Adam and born in sin; regenerated in Christ; and glorified for ever. Marvellous are the works of our God!

2. 'My substance (my being, my frame, my life) was known to you when I was conceived and formed in my mother's womb' (Jer. 1:5).

3. 'You saw me, loved me, knew me, and in your book of life and purpose my name was written and my life and days were recorded even when there were none' (John 10:14-16,27-29; Eph. 1:3-7). God has predestined all whom he has foreknown to be perfectly conformed to the image of his Son, before they were born, or even before the world began (Rom. 8:28-31). How shall a Jewish boy ever sit upon the throne of Egypt? God knows!

vv.17-18. **'How precious ... are thy thoughts unto me, O God!'** God knows our thoughts of ourselves and of him, and they are by nature only evil continually. But his thoughts towards us are love and grace. What can I say?

1. It is marvellous that God should even think upon us.

2. It is marvellous that his thoughts are not evil towards us.

3. It is more marvellous and precious that his thoughts towards us are more than the sand in the desert and on the ocean floor. I go to my bed rejoicing in thy mercies to me and **'When I awake, I am still with thee'**. Soon we shall lie down to sleep for the last time; and when we awake, we shall awake in his likeness (Ps. 17:15).

vv.19-22. Just as surely as God will redeem his elect, he will slay the wicked! Eternal death out of Christ is as sure as eternal life in Christ. These wicked men have two great offences: they speak against God; and they carelessly use his name in vain. This is done in religion as much as in the dens of iniquity. David adds, 'God's enemies are my enemies' (Rev. 19:1-3).

vv.23-24. 'I do not want to be among his enemies. I want to think reverently and thankfully of my God. I want to own, revere and praise his name. Lord, search me, try me, redeem me and lead me in the way of Christ, which is the way everlasting.' I must be led in that way, for by nature I neither know it nor desire it.

20. 'Praise the Lord, O my soul'

Psalm 146

I am troubled that these great and meaningful words, 'Praise the Lord', 'Hallelujah' and 'Blessed Jesus' have become mere flippant and meaningless, religious bywords. Men ought to exercise great care in the use of the name of our great God, lest we be guilty of taking his name in vain (Eccles. 5:1-2; Exod. 20:7).

v.1. **'Praise the Lord, O my soul.'** True praise is not lip-service, but it is from the heart and soul (Matt. 15:7-8). Let us be certain that our lips speak the true feelings of our hearts, or let us not speak at all before the Lord. The Lord can be (and is) praised in heart without a word being uttered. Hannah demonstrated this (1 Sam. 1:9-15; Rom. 8:26).

v.2. **'While I live, will I praise the Lord.'** I have good reason to praise the Lord while I live, for if I live, I live by his will and pleasure. He gives life and he sustains life (Acts 17:28; Job 14:5). I have greater reason to praise the Lord if I live spiritually. It is by his will in Christ Jesus that I am born again (John 1:12-13; Eph. 2:1). I will be able in glory to praise him as he ought to be praised, for I shall awake with his likeness (Rev. 5:9-12; Ps. 17:15). **'I will sing praises unto my God while I have any being'**, which is for ever!

v.3. 'Put not your trust in men, no matter how high they are in politics, economics or religion. In man there is no help, hope, or salvation.' David discourages the people from putting any trust or confidence in him, in their nobles, in any man, or in themselves. There is no good in the flesh and it has been proved under every circumstance. For a man to put spiritual confidence in another man is like a beggar looking to another beggar for food, or a blind man reaching for the hand of another blind man to guide him (Phil. 3:3).

v.4. Why not put trust and confidence in men? David gives several reasons.

'His breath goeth forth,' and he dies. Man is so frail and impotent, that he dies for want of a little air. No matter how much he knows, has, nor how high he stands, he will die when he stops breathing.

'He returneth to his earth.' The dust is his; he was made from it and he will return to it. What can one so frail give to me?

'In that very day [of death] **his thoughts perish.'** All of his thoughts, plans, programmes and expectations perish with him. He withers like the grass and wilts like the flower, and nothing he thought remains; only the Word of God abides for ever! Our thoughts are ours, not God's (Isa. 55:8).

v.5. **'Happy** [blessed] **is he that hath the God of Jacob for his help, whose hope is in the Lord his God.'** Who is this God of Jacob?

1. He is the God of covenant mercies. 'Jacob have I loved, but Esau have I hated' (Rom. 9:11-13). His mercies are sure because he chose us and predestined us to be like Christ (Rom. 8:29-31; Eph. 1:3-7).

2. He is the God of revelation. As he revealed himself to Jacob at Bethel, blessed him and changed his name, so he reveals himself to us and gives us his name.

3. He is the Lord Jehovah, our God. He is a 'just God and a Saviour' (Isa. 45:20-25). In Christ he can be both just and justifier (Rom. 3:25-26).

4. He is our help (a very present help in time of trouble) and our hope (Ps. 130:7).

v.6. We cannot trust men, but we can wisely trust our God, for he who made the heavens can make a heaven for us and make us in Christ fit for heaven. He who made the earth can preserve us while we are on the earth and supply all our needs. He who made the seas and all the mysteries therein can keep us in trouble and make a way for us to pass over. Concerning all of our circumstances, we can say, 'Jehovah Shammah,' the Lord is present. He **'keepeth truth for ever'**. He is true to his promises, true to his covenant, to his Word and to his Son. 'I am the Lord; I change not.' His gifts and calling are without change (Mal. 3:6; Rom. 11:29).

v.7. We may trust our way to the Lord because he **'executeth judgement for the oppressed'**. He is the just judge. What a joy to commit our care, our defence and our future to such a ruler! Not only does he mete out justice, but he **'giveth food to the hungry'**. All food, both physical and spiritual, comes from God. To complete the triple blessing, David says, 'He sets the prisoner free.' Justice, bread and liberty! If the Son shall make you free, you are free indeed — free from sin's penalty, power and some day from its very presence.

vv.8-9. Note that five times the name 'Jehovah' is repeated in verses 7 to 9. It is as God, our Saviour, as God in Christ Jesus, that he **'looseth the prisoners'** of sin, death and judgement; that he **'openeth the eyes of the blind'** to see his glory in the face of Christ; that he **'raiseth them that are bowed down'** in distress, despair, sickness and old age; that he **'loveth the righteous'** (none are righteous in themselves, but they are clothed in the righteousness of the Redeemer); and **'preserveth the strangers'**. His people do not belong to this world but, like Abraham, are strangers and pilgrims. If we are enabled by his grace to see that all God's favour, mercies and grace towards us are in Christ Jesus, our substitute and Saviour, we can lay hold of every promise in these verses and rest there; we can find happiness and joy. In Christ all things are ours (1 Cor. 3:21-23) and all things work together for our good (Rom. 8:28), but **'The way of the wicked** [and the unbeliever] **he turneth upside down'**.

v.10. Trust in men and perish; trust in Jehovah and live, for Jehovah shall reign for ever. He is the same yesterday, today and for ever and **'unto all generations. Praise ye the Lord!'**

21. Wisdom in Christ

Proverbs 8

This chapter contains the instructions of wisdom, or Christ; for he is the wisdom of God and he is made unto us wisdom and understanding (1 Cor. 1:30; 1 John 5:20).

v.1. Wisdom cries, or proclaims and preaches, the everlasting gospel, which directs men in the way of peace, acceptance and eternal happiness. Truth does not whisper, like the tempter, nor seek a dark corner, but boldly puts forth its voice that all may hear. The truth of Christ will stand the light.

vv.2-3. Our Lord's voice is heard in his Word, from his prophets (Heb. 1:1), in his own person and by his apostles and preachers. The gospel is to be proclaimed to all men from **'the high places'** ('He went up into a mountain', Matt. 5:1), between the paths, or where the roads cross, **'at the gates'** of the temple, in **'the city'** and in private homes (Mark 16:15-16).

v.4. The good news of reconciliation and redemption in Christ Jesus is to **'men'** — fallen sons of Adam! It is not just to noble men, wise men, or good men, but it is to all men (1 Cor. 1:26-31; Matt. 11:28). 'Ho, everyone that thirsteth, come ye to the waters' (Isa. 55:1). The voice of Christ is to all the **'sons of man'** (Rev. 5:9).

v.5. The gospel of Christ Jesus, salvation by Christ, is the wisdom of God in a mystery (1 Cor. 2:7-10). It is the highest wisdom to know Christ and him crucified. All men by nature are simple and are fools without understanding of spiritual truth, but in Christ the wisdom and understanding of God's will and purpose are revealed to them (1 Cor. 1:18-24).

v.6. The things of the gospel excel all knowledge and light (1 Cor. 12:31; Heb. 1:4; 8:6), all persons, all covenants and all laws. They are excellent in their author, their content and their promises. He speaks right things — agreeable to the very righteousness of God, consistent with the justice of God (Rom. 3:25-26) and manifesting all the attributes of God (Ps. 85:8-13).

vv.7-8. His mouth speaks nothing but the truth of God (Heb. 1:1-3), for he is the truth. All the doctrines of Christ are agreeable to the Scriptures and to the character of God. The gospel of Christ is called the word of truth (Eph. 1:13). The words of his mouth are agreeable to righteousness! The necessity of righteousness for eternal life, the insufficiency of man's righteousness and the excellency of Christ's righteousness — this is the righteousness of which he speaks (Rom. 3:21-22).

v.9. When a man's understanding is enlightened by the Spirit of God, when he is blessed of God to have ears to hear, eyes to see and a heart to understand the gospel, the mysteries of the gospel are plain and right to him. The Bible is a sealed book and the gospel is foolishness to all natural men, learned or unlearned, until God gives understanding (2 Cor. 4:3-6; 1 Cor. 2:9-14).

vv.10-11. The wisdom of Christ and the knowledge of God in Christ are more to be desired than all that the world can offer. Nothing can be even slightly compared with the riches of God in Christ (Heb. 11:24-26).

v.12. All the treasures of wisdom, knowledge and judgement dwell in Christ. He knows the hearts of men, their thoughts, schemes and devices. He knows the wiles and craftiness of Satan and makes them known to his people, so that they are not deceived (Matt. 24:24).

v.13. The fear and reverence of the Lord make his people to hate evil, even when it is found in themselves, especially pride and arrogance (Prov. 3:7; 16:18; 6:16-17). A froward mouth speaks things contrary to the truth, to the gospel and to the good of his people.

vv.14-16. These words are all of Christ! He is the counsel of God and the Counsellor (Isa. 9:6). He is wisdom and understanding, the fountain, author and giver of understanding. He has all strength, power and authority (Matt. 28:18; John 17:2). By him all things consist, exist and are held together. Even kings, princes, judges and magistrates rule by his permission and pleasure, and they are accountable to him (Rom. 13:1; Prov. 21:1).

v.17. Christ Jesus loves those who love him, for he loved them *before* they loved him, and they love him *because* he loved them (1 John 4:10,19). Those who seek Christ are those who see their need of Christ and know the worth and glory of Christ. They shall seek him early and find him.

vv.18-21. True riches and the honour that comes from God are found in our Redeemer; all else fades away with the fashion of this world. **'I lead'** them in the paths of righteousness as a shepherd leads his sheep, that those who love him shall **'inherit substance'**, that is, the reality of life, glory and riches, as opposed to the vain, shadowy, temporary things of this life.

vv.22-31. Read these verses carefully and note the eternality of the Lord Jesus Christ, his glory and majesty, his oneness with the Father and the affection the Father has for him (John 3:35). If we can grasp the person, power, position and glory that Christ has with the Father, then we can rest and hope with great assurance for the glory that shall be ours in him (John 17:20-24).

vv.32-34. Now, therefore, with all this in mind, 'Hear my voice and receive my words' (John 6:68). 'To whom shall we go?' He has the words of life. Blessed is the man that hears and refuses not his gospel (Rom. 4:7-8; Ps. 65:4). 'Blessed is the man who hears me and waits at the school doors' to go in first to hear Christ, the Teacher, and to sit at his feet as Mary of old.

vv.35-36. Oh, the happiness of those who find him! And who can tell the misery of those who do not?

22. The conclusion of the whole matter

Ecclesiastes 1 - 2

The principal doctrine of these chapters is that the world and all things in it and of it are vain things. 'The fashion of this world passeth away' (1 Cor. 7:31). Our Lord said, 'What shall it profit a man, if he shall gain the whole world, and lose his own soul?' (Mark 8:36). What remains of this world (its labours, its glory, its relationships, its titles of honour, its wealth) after a man is dead? Nothing at all! These all die with him. He goes naked out of this world as he came into it.

1:12. Solomon was God's preacher first and King of Israel second. Being **'the Preacher'**, he was qualified to teach and instruct others, and being **'king over Israel'**, he did not lack for money, power, or opportunity to search into and participate in all that the world afforded. If there was anyone who could speak first-hand of the vanities of the world and the true riches of God, it was the preacher-king, Solomon (1 Kings 3:12; 4:29-31).

1:17-18. **'I gave my heart to know** [seek and search out] **wisdom.'** He made himself master of the arts and sciences; he got knowledge of trades and vocations; he studied politics, philosophy, education and history. He pursued human wisdom — not just superficial knowledge, but he penetrated into the depths of all that men can know.

His conclusion? Behold all is vanity and **'vexation of spirit'**. **'In much wisdom is much grief.'** The more a man knows, the more he wants to know, and the more sensible he becomes of his ignorance and the insufficiency of such knowledge to make him happy. All that worldly knowledge and wisdom can do is cause vexation of spirit and promote grief and sorrow. The wisdom of men is foolishness with God and only serves to take a man farther from God and promote misery of soul.

2:1-3. Solomon reasoned within himself that since he could not find happiness in natural wisdom, he would seek it in **'pleasure'**. Sordid lusts and sensual pleasure are not meant here, for Solomon was too wise and too godly a man to indulge in low, lewd behaviour. No particulars are given, but it is reasonable that he decided to give himself to laughter, entertainment, foolishness (taking nothing seriously) and feasting. By 'giving himself to wine', he does not mean drunkenness, but giving himself to the so-called 'good life' of banquetry, entertaining, living luxuriously and keeping back nothing that would give his flesh pleasure and comfort (1 Kings 4:22-23).

His conclusion: **'Behold, this also is vanity.'** He said of laughter, entertainment and pleasure that **'It is mad,'** and asked, what good does it do? There is no solid and substantial happiness nor lasting peace in any of it. It is a road that has no end and a hunger and thirst that are never satisfied.

2:4-11. Solomon then turned to **'great works'**. He did not spend his time with small projects or trifling things. Since he was the richest, wisest and most powerful man in the world, he made great works. His houses, his gardens and orchards, his lakes, his treasures, his staff of servants and his orchestras would be the envy of any person who ever lived (vv.9-10). So he was great, wise and wealthy; then he looked on all these things and on all his labour, **'and, behold, all was vanity and vexation of spirit'**. There was no real profit in any of it!

2:12-23. Wisdom is better than foolishness, but the wise man, like the fool, dies and leaves it all behind. There is no remembrance of the wise or the great; they all die alike. Therefore, he hated life and he hated his labour; for in itself, it is vanity and affords no peace or rest. Here is the conclusion of the whole matter. There is an answer and there is a good life here and a greater life hereafter, if these things are put in their proper places.

2:24. Is it wrong for a man to study, to improve his mind, acquire an education, become a teacher, a mechanic, a builder or an artist?

Is it wrong to marry, build a house, plant a garden, raise a family and enjoy our friends and life? No! **'There is nothing better for a man, than that he should eat and drink and ... enjoy... his labour,'** for it is all from the hand of God! 'A man can receive nothing, except it be given him from heaven' (John 3:27; 1 Cor. 4:7; James 1:17). All that God gives us is to be received with thanksgiving and enjoyed.

2:25. 'Who knows that more than I?' asks Solomon. 'God made me wise, God made me king and God gave me what I have.'

2:26. Here is the key: **'God giveth to a man that is good in his sight wisdom, and knowledge, and joy.'**
Who is the man that is good in his sight? 'There is none good,' the Scriptures tell us. This is the man who is righteous and good in Christ through faith (Rom. 3:20-23; 2 Cor. 5:21).

God gives him that wisdom, knowledge and joy that enable him to properly enjoy the good of his labour. He is not spiritually wise by nature, but by the regenerating grace of God. 'I am what I am by the grace of God.' What he knows and what he has are gifts of God!

God gives the believer *wisdom* (1 Cor. 1:24-30; Col. 2:3). This wisdom enables him to understand the mysteries of grace and life, to understand what true riches are, to remember that a man's life is not in food and drink, to look on things that are not seen and to hold lightly to all material possessions and relationships, for they are temporary.

God gives the believer *knowledge* (2 Tim. 1:12; John 17:3). He knows the source of all mercies and blessings; he knows how to use them and not be used by them; he knows how to be a generous and good steward; he knows how to be abased and to abound; he knows that the earth is the Lord's!

5. God gives the believer true *joy* (Rom. 5:11). Our joy is not in this world, nor in anything it holds; our joy and rejoicing are in our Lord Jesus Christ. We rejoice that our names are in his book and we are in him (Phil. 3:1-3).

23. 'Remember now thy Creator'

Ecclesiastes 12

'Behold, the Lord's hand is not shortened, that it cannot save; neither his ear heavy, that it cannot hear' (Isa. 59:1). Our Lord is able to save to the uttermost those that come to God by him, young or old. All men and women ought to seek the Lord at all times! God commands all to repent and believe the record that he has given concerning his Son. But this chapter deals with things as they are, not as they ought to be. It is a fact that the overwhelming majority of people who do not seek the Lord early will spend old age in the gall of bitterness and die without God and without hope. Those who learn the grace of God in Christ early in life live out their days on earth walking with God in peace, resting in his good providence, and die with a good hope of life eternal.

v.1. **'Remember now thy Creator in the days of thy youth.'** 'Thy Creator' is the Father, Son and Holy Spirit. One cannot remember, worship, or know one without the other. Our creation, existence and life are attributed to Father, Son and Spirit (Read Mal. 2:10; John 1:1-4; Job 33:4).

This God (1 John 5:5-7) should be *remembered.* The word 'remember' is to recognize, think upon and be mindful of. This is what the thief had in mind when he asked to be remembered by Christ when he came into his kingdom. Remembering our Creator is not a casual thought, or an indifferent glance, but setting him always before us in love, fear and worship and never forgetting him (Ps. 146:1-2).

1. We are mindful that there is a God of great and glorious perfections (omnipotent, omniscient, omnipresent, holy, just and true) who will judge the world in righteousness (Isa. 46:9-13).

2. We are mindful that God is, in Christ Jesus, a God gracious and merciful, pardoning iniquity and sin by his obedience and death.

3. We are mindful that the end for which we are made is to glorify him (Rev. 4:11). If we are saved, resurrected on that great day and conformed to the image of Christ, it will be by his grace, according to his mercy, through his own work and for his glory (1 Cor. 1:30-31).

We are to be mindful of him in the days of youth, which are the best and choicest days. God is worthy of the first-fruits, when our bodies are healthy, our minds are quick and our souls capable of being enlarged. To delay our worship of him is ungrateful, for he is the giver of every gift, and foolish, for no man can be sure of tomorrow (Prov. 27:1; James 4:13-16).

'The evil days' that are sure to come mean the days of old age. They are called the 'evil days', not because sins of old age are any more evil than sins of youth, but because old age is attended by trouble, disease and affliction. There are weakness of body, decay of intellect and inability to discern, desire or put together the hopes and mysteries of spiritual truth. Men and women who live their lives without God come to old age with no pleasure in looking back, no pleasure in their present circumstances and certainly no pleasure in thinking of death and eternity! Contrary to this, Paul viewed the past, present and future with joy and delight (2 Tim. 4:6-8).

vv.2-7. Solomon describes the infirmities of old age and the troubles that come upon us, in order to encourage the young to seek the Lord early.

'The sun ... the light ... the moon' and **'the stars'** will be darkened. This is the understanding, mind, judgement and memory. All of these are greatly impaired or lost in old age.

'The clouds return after the rain.' In youth troubles come, but then there is sunshine and a clear day; in old age, as soon as one cloud arises and departs, another follows.

v.3. **'The keepers of the house shall tremble.'** The house is the body, and the keepers are the arms and hands, which in old age become weak.

'The strong men' are the thighs, legs and feet, which have supported the house.

'**The grinders**', which '**cease because they are few**', are the teeth.

'**Those that look out of the windows**', and which are '**darkened**', are the eyes.

v.4. '**The doors shall be shut**' must refer to the lips, which are opened for speaking and eating, but in the aged they are shut more than opened for either.

They '**shall rise up at the voice of the bird**'. Old men usually retire early and rise early.

'**The daughters of music shall be brought low.**' What are the instruments of music? The lungs, throat, mouth, teeth and lips, all of which are weakened by old age.

v.5. '**They shall be afraid of ... high**' places, such as mountains, hills and towers, because of the feebleness of their limbs.

'**The almond tree shall flourish.**' This is the white hair which looks like an almond tree in bloom.

'**The grasshopper**' is a very light thing, but the lightest load is a burden to the aged.

'**Desire shall fail**'; desire for almost everything is weakened by old age.

'**Man goeth to his long home.**' The grave is the home of the body.

v.6. '**The silver cord**' is the bond between soul and body. '**The golden bowl**' is the brain, which stops functioning and '**the pitcher ... broken at the fountain**' is the heart, which is the fountain of life.

vv.7-8. The body, which is dust, shall return to the earth and the spirit or soul shall return to God who gave it. Now when you consider all this vanity of the world and the flesh, is it not wise to remember, be mindful of and seek to know the living God with whom we have to do? How foolish to invest all in decaying flesh!

vv.9-14. '**The preacher was wise.**' God taught him and he taught the people the words of God.

'**The preacher sought to find out acceptable words,**' not mere words, but words of truth, delight and promise.

The preacher's words are like **'goads'**, sharpened sticks, to prick sinners in heart and direct them in the true way, and also like **'nails'** to fasten us to Christ.

'The conclusion of the whole matter', the sum and substance of the whole book, is reduced to two things — the fear of God and obedience to him, which are urged from the consideration of who he is and what he will do!

24. 'My beloved is mine and I am his'

Song of Solomon 2

Solomon, next to our Lord Jesus, was the greatest son of wisdom that the church of God has ever known (1 Kings 4:29-32).

God blessed him with 'largeness of heart'. His love and affection are evidenced by his many wives, who were his undoing. But true understanding and love will always be found together.

Though Solomon spoke over 3,000 proverbs and 1,500 songs, 'The Song of Solomon' is his most profound and beautiful work. God used the man of greatest wisdom to write on the greatest subject — love: the love of Christ and his church!

Other writings of Solomon are more obvious and open to common understanding, but, as none entered into the holy of holies except the high priest, so none can enter into the beauties and mysteries of the Song of Solomon except those who know and love the Bridegroom — Christ Jesus! (Read Titus 1:15).

In this chapter there is a conversation between Christ and his church, in which they alternately set forth the excellencies of each other and express their affection for, and the delight and pleasure they take in, each other's company.

v.1. These are the words of Christ concerning himself. He compares himself to **'the rose'** and **'the lily'** for fragrance and beauty (Isa. 35:1-2). He is to be preferred above all, for he is above all (Phil. 2:9-11).

v.2. He says that his church is **'the lily among thorns'**, beauty among ugliness! He calls the church **'my love'** and, though she is growing among thorns and unfruitful tares, he declares her beauty and his love for her.

v.3. The church declares that Christ is like **'an apple tree'** among the barren trees of the forest. It is said that the apple tree is a symbol of love, under which lovers sat (S. of S. 8:5). To send or throw an apple meant love. Christ is our apple tree for shade, rest and fruit.

v.4. **'He brought me to the banqueting house.'** By his invincible grace he sought me, called me and brought me. The house of God is the place where we feed upon him and his Word. All that the church needs is satisfied there. Our reason for being there is because he loved us (1 John 4:10,19). We are not guests only; we are the bride.

v.5. **'Stay me'**, or 'sustain me, with vessels of wine poured out and comfort me with tokens and reminders of love (**"apples"**), for I am sick with love'; that is, 'I am eagerly desirous to know more of his love' (Phil. 3:10). The church never gets enough of Christ Jesus.

v.6. He loves his church, he feeds his church, he comforts his church and he holds and supports his church with both hands, as a lover embraces his beloved. He will not let her go nor suffer her to leave (Heb. 13:5-6).

v.7. There is much debate about who is speaking here, whether Christ of the church or the church of Christ, but one thing is clear — he is sovereign! No force, power, nor person can disturb him or his church **'till he please'** (Ps. 115:1-3).

vv.8-9. The church relates how she heard the voice of Christ (John 10:27) and had a sight of him as a young deer on the hills and mountains, at some distance (as in the shadows and types of the Old Testament), then nearer, behind her wall and through the lattices (in part and through a glass dimly — 1 Cor. 13:9,12).

v.10. The voice of Christ (which the church heard) gave her a call to come away with him. **'My love, my fair one'** (terms of endearment), 'rise up from where you are, from what you are doing and whom you are with, and come with me' (Matt. 11:28-30). He called outwardly by his Word and inwardly by his Spirit (Gal. 1:15; James 1:18; 1 Thess. 2:13-14). His call is an effectual call. None who hear his voice in grace and mercy will refuse to come to him.

vv.11-13. Before he came to us in love and before we heard his voice, it was like winter in our souls, dark with sin, cold and barren and dead. We were under judgement for sin and driven by the winds of Satan's temptations. The winter is past; it is summer in our hearts. We have been redeemed by his blood and are free to go in and out. The flowers bloom, the birds sing and the sun of righteousness shines upon us.

v.14. The church is called his **'dove'**, partly for her temperament (because she is harmless, innocent and beautiful in his grace) and partly for her dove-like condition (because she is weak and exposed to persecution and trial and given to mourning). Therefore, she is called to hide in him, **'the rock'**, and in his **'secret places'** for protection. 'Cast your care upon him.' He says to the church, 'Let me see your face in communion and worship; let me hear your voice in prayer and praise, for your voice is sweet to me and your countenance comely.'

v.15. 'Put away the little foxes' — our flesh, thoughts, infirmities, that war against the soul, for, like tender grapes, we are children beset within and without by terrible foes (Eph. 6:12).

v.16. These two statements are strong and positive.

'My beloved is mine.'
    1. By divine decree he is mine. 'Thou gavest them me' (John 17:6-10).
    2. By a living union he is my vine, head and husband.
    3. By faith he is mine, for I have believed and received him according to God's Word.
    4. By an affectionate relationship he is mine. He is **'my beloved'**.

'I am his.' I belong to him.
    1. The Father gave me to him (John 6:37-39).
    2. He purchased me on the cross of Calvary. 'Ye are not your own, ye are bought with a price' (1 Cor. 6:19-20).

v.17. 'He is mine and I am his until the morning of that great and blessed day of resurrection when all shadows shall flee away.'

25. 'What is thy beloved more than another beloved?'

Song of Solomon 5:9-16

v.9. This question is put to the church of the Lord Jesus — **'O thou fairest among women'** — the same title Christ gives her in 1:8.

Every soul has a beloved, an object of worship, something or someone in which to glory, rejoice and to enjoy. With some it is the world (its riches, materialism and honours); with others it is pleasure and the applause of men; with others it is near and dear family and friends; with others it is religion and works of righteousness; and with most it is self!

A true believer in Christ Jesus worships, loves, rejoices and glories only in Christ Jesus — his beloved! Christ is preferred above all persons, possessions and pursuits.

The world and professors of religion (because they are ignorant of Christ's excellencies) ask the church, 'What is your beloved more than our beloved?' These next verses contain the church's answer to the question.

v.10. **'My beloved is white and ruddy.'** White denotes his purity and holiness, his divine nature, the brightness of the Father's glory, full of grace and truth. 'He knew no sin.' Ruddy, or red, indicates his human nature, partaker of our flesh and blood, his strength in suffering, his bloody sacrifice for the sins of his people.

He is **'the chiefest among ten thousand'**. Among all creatures, angels, or men, he is exalted. A certain number is used for an uncertain. There are kings, but he is the King of kings. There are priests, but he is a priest for ever. There are names, but his is a name above every name (Phil. 2:9-11).

v.11. **'His head is as the most fine gold,'** not in respect to his hair, which is black, but by reason of the crown he wears. He is the

sovereign, almighty King, who rules over all (John 17:2; Matt.
28:18; Col. 1:16-18). Our Lord is not *going to be* King; he *is* King
of creation, providence and salvation, by reason of the Father's
decrees and his death (Ps. 2:6; Rom. 14:9).

'His locks are bushy, and black as a raven.' Two things seem
to be indicated here — his beauty and his eternal youth. Who can
describe the perfections of the glorified man, Christ Jesus? John's
vision on Patmos gives us a glimpse (Rev. 1:12-17). His beauty and
youth are unchanging, infinite, immaculate — the very image of
God's holiness, brightness and glory. And one day we shall be like
him (Ps. 17:15).

v.12. **'His eyes are as the eyes of doves.'** To the rebel and the
unbeliever his countenance and eyes may be fierce and condemning, but to his own beloved his eyes are gentle and clear as if
'washed with milk'. He looks upon us in total love, forgiveness and
acceptance. Someone said, 'The eyes are the windows of the soul,
which reveal the true thoughts.' Then I can rest and rejoice, for his
eyes are gentle and compassionate. His thoughts towards me are
love. His eyes are **'fitly set'** or unchanging towards me (Mal. 3:6;
Rom. 11:29).

v.13. **'His cheeks are as a bed of spices, as sweet flowers.'** This
just has to indicate the rest, comfort and assurance the believer feels
in the presence of his Lord. Leaning upon his cheek and reclining in
his everlasting arms are like lying upon a bed of sweet spices and
soft, sweet-smelling flowers. No rain, no storm, no wind can disturb
my rest (Matt. 11:28; 1 Peter 5:7).

'His lips like lilies, dropping sweet smelling myrrh.' This is
indeed his grace and mercy, which flow from his lips continuously.
Sweet to my ears, to my heart and to my taste are the words of my
Lord. His promises are sure and precious. His lips shall call my
name, assure me of his love and intercede for me. He has no words
of condemnation, but words of life (Rom. 8:1).

v.14. **'His hands are as gold rings set with the beryl.'** The hands
are for action and distribution, by which he gives gifts and graces to
his own, and being the Lord of all, he is rich and generous (Phil.
4:19). All of my needs he supplies. He has blessed us with all
spiritual blessings (Eph. 1:3).

'**His belly is as bright ivory overlaid with sapphires.**' Some believe these words describe the overall beauty of his whole body; some believe it has reference to his priestly garments (the royal girdle of righteousness), and others the compassion of Christ to his church. His love is like ivory for the excellency of it, like sapphires for the firmness and duration of it, as well as for the sincerity of it. We know that the word 'belly' is used in Scripture for the innermost part of a person (John 7:38; Ps. 31:9). There is merit in all these thoughts.

v.15. '**His legs are as pillars of marble, set upon sockets of fine gold.**' The legs support the body, and this denotes the strength and power of our Lord Jesus to bear up and carry what has been laid upon him — the covenant of grace, the mediatorial kingdom, the redemption and the reward of his people. He is able to save (Heb. 7:25). He is able to keep (Jude 24-25). He is able to comfort (Heb. 2:18).

'**His countenance is as Lebanon, excellent as the cedars.**' Lebanon was a goodly mountain north of Judea; the cedars of Lebanon were the choicest and were preferable to all others. Christ's appearance and person are majestic, stately and durable, like the choicest cedars, pleasant to the eyes. In all comparisons he is more excellent, which is the theme of the book of Hebrews (Heb. 1:4).

v.16. '**His mouth is most sweet.**' This is repeated from verse 13, because his words are one of the principal parts of his beauty. All that proceeds from his mouth is most sweet — his gospel, his commandments, his promises, his doctrine.

'**Yea, he is altogether lovely.**' If I have neglected any part of him, or failed in any respect to define him, I add, 'He is altogether lovely'! There is nothing about him or his person that is not exquisitely beautiful.

'**This is my beloved and this is my friend,**' my rich, powerful, faithful, everlasting and unchangeable Friend.

26. 'Come now and let us reason together'

Isaiah 1:1-20

Isaiah was one of the sixteen prophets whose writings are contained in the Holy Scriptures. There are more testimonies and quotations in the New Testament taken out of Isaiah than out of all the other prophets. Isaiah so fully describes the person, offices, sufferings and kingdom of the Lord Jesus Christ that some have called him 'the fifth evangelist', and his book 'the Gospel according to Isaiah'.

v.1. His prophecy is called a **'vision'** because the truth that God revealed to him was as clear to his mind as bodily objects are to men's eyes. He foresaw and he foretold (2 Peter 1:20-21; 2 Tim. 3:16; 1 Peter 1:10-11).

v.2. Isaiah calls upon the whole creation to hear the Lord's charge against Judah and Jerusalem. The Lord said, 'I have made them my people' (Deut. 7:6-8), 'I blessed and sustained them above all nations, I gave them the law and the prophets, and they have rebelled against me.'

v.3. They are more stupid and ungrateful than beasts. We hear the sayings, 'Stubborn as an ass,' and 'Dumb as an ox', but even these dumb beasts acknowledge and obey their masters and benefactors. 'But my people do not know me, consider or think upon me, reverence or obey me.'

v.4. They are **'laden with iniquity'**. The word 'laden' means heavy, full and thick, as full of sin as an egg or a sponge is full (Rom. 3:12-18).

'A seed of evildoers' — children of rebels (Rom. 5:12), who have forsaken the Lord and gone their own way (Isa. 53:6). God is angry (Ps. 7:11; Heb. 10:30-31).

v.5. They are so depraved and rebellious that even afflictions and the judgements of God have no effect upon them (Amos 4:6,9-11). 'Why should I chasten and correct you?' You are so mentally warped (**'the ... head is sick'**) and spiritually dead (**'the heart faint'**), that even correction brings out rebellion. Judgement will not produce repentance in a depraved sinner (Rev. 16:9; Rom. 2:4).

v.6. Here is the result of Adam's fall, a description of total depravity, the true condition of fallen flesh! From the very soles of our feet to the hair on top of our heads, there is no life, no truth, no light, no goodness in us (Rom. 7:18; 8:8; Eph. 2:1-3). These wounds and sores of sin are open and ugly and have no remedy.

vv.7-8. Because of your rebellion and disobedience you lie desolate, destroyed by the enemy, bruised, broken and afflicted. You have no peace, rest, or happiness. Men without God are without hope, in this world or in the world to come (Eph. 2:12).

v.9. If the Lord of hosts, by his infinite grace and goodness, had not chosen a people from Adam's race, defeated our enemies in the person and work of his Son and called us effectually by his Spirit, no one would be saved. We would all have been cut off like the people of Sodom (Rom. 9:27-29). 'Salvation is of the Lord' in its origination (2 Thess. 2:13), in its execution (Gal. 4:4-5), in its application (Gal. 1:15), in its sustaining power (Jude 24-25) and in its ultimate perfection (Rev. 21:3-6).

vv.10-15. Here is a startling revelation! Believe it or not, these ungrateful, irreverent, totally depraved people make a pretence of being religious! They are inwardly wicked and outwardly religious (Matt. 23:25-28). They kept the outward forms, ceremonies and holy days, yet they did not love, obey, or worship God in their hearts. It is so often true that the less a man knows of God and the farther he departs from the true and living God, the more of the outward form of religion he adopts. The less the internal devotion, the more emphasis is placed on the external ceremony and the outward rules and regulations. Their outward show of piety, prayer, sacrifice and sabbaths was an abomination to God (Luke 16:15).

v.16. **'Wash you, make you clean.'** Notwithstanding their sacrifices and ceremonies, they were unclean (as all men are) and needed to be washed in the blood of Christ (Ps. 51:7; 1 John 1:7). The blood of animals cannot put away sin, nor can the deeds of the law or religious works.

'Put away the evil of your doings from before mine eyes.' Not only put away the doing of evil, but also the evil of doing, which is an attempt to be justified before the eyes of God by our doings (Rom. 10:1-4).

v.17. **'Learn to do well.'** These are the true works of righteousness that are produced by a right relationship with God in Christ Jesus (Gal. 5:22). Observing the ceremonies, sacrifices and sabbaths outwardly is meaningless, but a regenerated, renewed and cleansed heart will find delight in serving God and others.

v.18. God in grace proposes a conference, not to determine if we are sinners, nor the extent of our sins, but what is to be done about the matter. We *are* sinners and our sins are double-dyed, **'as scarlet'** and **'red like crimson'**. Only Christ can put away our sins by the sacrifice of himself (Heb. 9:26; 10:12-14).

vv.19-20. If you be made willing to come to Christ in repentance and faith, you shall eat the good of God's great land; if you refuse him, you shall be devoured, **'for the mouth of the Lord hath spoken it'**.

    1. Are we willing to own and confess our sins?

    2. Are we willing to repent of dead works and personal merit?

    3. Are we willing to call on God in Christ for mercy and grace?

    4. Are we willing to confess him and bow to him as Lord (Rom. 10:9-10)?

Then we shall be saved!

27. 'Here am I; send me'

Isaiah 6:1-8

Isaiah was a prophet of God who lived about 700 years before Christ came to earth in the flesh. He lived about 120 years and preached for about eighty-five of those years. He was a prophet in the days of Uzziah, Jotham, Ahaz and Hezekiah, kings of Judah.

v.1. **'In the year that king Uzziah died I saw also the Lord.'** Is there some connection between the death of King Uzziah and Isaiah's vision of God's holiness? Perhaps! Uzziah was a great and successful king whom Isaiah probably admired (2 Chron. 26:22). He did many great and notable things, but he became proud and presumptuous. His pride led him to the temple to offer incense to God, not through God's priest, but by his own hand. This is a denial of the holiness of God and the work of Christ, our great High Priest (2 Chron. 26:16-20). Christ is God's priest (typified by the Old Testament priesthood), and not even a king can come to God except through him (John 14:6). God judged Uzziah and he died a leper. When Uzziah died, Isaiah saw the Lord.

1. Isaiah saw the supreme glory of Christ. It was the enthroned Christ, the sovereign Christ of all authority and glory, for John wrote of this experience, 'When Isaiah saw his glory, he spoke of him' (see John 12:41).

2. Isaiah saw the victorious Christ, for he was sitting on a throne. Men and nations rush to and fro; we pace the floor and fret and worry. He sits amid complete order and purpose (Isa. 46:10-11; Ps. 110:1).

3. Isaiah saw the infinite glory of Christ, for he is **'high and lifted up'**. His name and throne are above every name and throne. 'None can stay his hand, or say unto him, What doest thou?' (Dan. 4:35; Phil. 2:9-11).

4. Isaiah saw the universal glory of Christ. His glory and presence **'filled the temple'**. 'Christ is all, and in all' (Col. 3:11). Every revelation of God to human eye, ear or heart is Jesus Christ (John 1:18). Isaiah saw Christ, the Lord, exalted King of kings and Lord of lords!

v.2. Around the throne Isaiah saw the seraphim. Who are these seraphim? There are many opinions, such as heavenly creatures, or angels, or perhaps (in figurative language) the true ministers of Christ.

1. They cover their faces in modesty and humility before the Lord, for they are less than the least, unworthy to be ministers, and the chief of sinners.
2. They cover their feet, conscious of the imperfection of their walk, conduct and ways. 'Oh, wretched man that I am!'
3. With two wings they fly in haste to declare the truth of his glorious person and work.

vv.3-4. What is their cry? **'Holy, holy, holy, is the Lord of hosts.'** The chief attribute of God is his holiness. God is love, God is just, God is merciful, but 'Holy and reverend is his name' (Ps. 111:9). All that God is and does must be in agreement with his holiness. Nowhere is the holiness of God revealed more clearly than at Calvary, when his holiness demanded and carried out the death of his Son to redeem a people (Rom. 3:25-26). The whole earth is his; all that is in it and all creation shall serve his glory (Rev. 4:11).

v.5. What was Isaiah's response to this revelation of God's presence and holiness?

He saw *himself*. 'I am undone and ruined; I am a sinful man; I am reduced to silence.' A man may look at others and say, 'I thank thee, I am not like other men.' He may look at the written law and say, 'I am blameless.' But when a man is exposed to the absolute holiness and righteousness of God, he must cry, **'Woe is me!'**

He saw the *evil of his heart and mouth*. Unclean lips speak from an unclean heart. The lips are the outlet of the heart.

He saw the *total ruin of the human race* (Rom. 3:10-19; Ps. 14:2-3). The twofold cry of the Word, of the gospel, of those who have seen the Lord is, first, 'All flesh is grass' and, secondly, 'Behold your God' (Isa. 40:6,9). The sinfulness of sin, the inability of the flesh and the need of sovereign mercy are only discovered in the light of God's holiness. Job experienced this (Job 42:5-6) and so shall all whom God is pleased to bring to a saving knowledge of Christ Jesus.

vv.6-7. God revealed to Isaiah, the sinner, his mercy and grace. When he saw the holiness of God, realized his corruption and evil and confessed his sinfulness and inability, there followed the application of mercy and grace in Christ. Self-judgement always precedes forgiveness (1 John 1:8-10). Grace is only for the guilty: Christ died only for the ungodly (1 Tim. 1:15; Rom. 5:6-8).

The seraph who came to him is the minister of the gospel, who is sent from God and comes to men (John 1:6-7). God sent Philip to the eunuch (Acts 8:29-30).

The **'live coal in his hand'** is the glorious gospel of the Lord Jesus Christ — his word of grace, the good news of mercy (Rom. 10:13-15; Eph. 1:13). The gospel is the power of God unto salvation (Rom. 1:16-17).

The altar of fire from which the live coal was taken is the sacrifice of Christ, our Lord. The Passover lamb was roasted on the altar of fire as our Lord Jesus (who is our Passover) was sacrificed for us. He endured the fire of God's wrath for our sins (2 Cor. 5:21). The pardon of sin, the cleansing, the power of God to redeem, come from the blood of Christ at Calvary (Heb. 10:12-17).

'He laid it upon my mouth.' That cleansing, purging fire of Calvary, the blood of the Son of God, actually met our sins, came in contact with all our iniquity, engaged to purge, burn out and eradicate all our transgressions (Isa. 53:4-6). 'He bore our sins.'

'Thine iniquity is taken away, and thy sin purged.' 'Your sin is completely atoned for and forgiven.' God said, 'I will remember their sins no more.' How can this be? Only in Christ, our substitute! God can be holy, just and righteous and justify us in Christ only. He obeyed the law, giving us a perfect righteousness (Rom. 5:19), and he died, 'the just for the unjust,' to bring us to God (1 Peter 3:18). 'Mercy and truth are met together; righteousness and peace have kissed each other' at Calvary (Ps. 85:10).

v.8. Who will go with the message of substitution and satisfaction through the person and work of Christ? Only the man whose lips have been touched by experience with that fire from the altar. **'Here am I; send me.'** I know, have experienced and love that gospel.

28. Jesus Christ — the mighty God

Isaiah 9:6-7

We have before us the greatest of all subjects, yet the most difficult and mysterious — the incarnation of God! God became a man. God took on himself 'the form of a servant, and was made in the likeness of men' (Phil. 2:5-8; 1 Tim. 3:16). The gift of Christ is called 'unspeakable' and the riches of Christ are called 'unsearchable' (2 Cor. 9:15; Eph. 3:8).

The Ancient of Days became an infant of days; he who made woman was made of a woman; God who is spirit actually became flesh and dwelt among us (John 1:14).

In the same breath that the prophet calls him a child, he calls him 'Counsellor' and 'everlasting Father'. The warrior's garments are rolled in blood, yet he is the Prince of peace. He is a 'man of sorrows' (Isa. 53:3), yet he is the mighty God. He is 'rejected of men' (Isa. 53:3), yet the government is on his shoulders. There are no contradictions here. Every word is true, but it is not learned by research and reason — only by revelation (1 Cor. 2:9-10,14). As Scripture is only interpreted in the light of Scripture, so:

1. There is no seeing Christ except in his own light (John 1:18).

2. He is the lesson learned, yet he himself is the teacher.

3. He is the one to whom we look and the light by which we see.

4. He is not only the tabernacle, the priest and the mercy-seat, but he is the sacrifice and the one to whom it is offered.

1. **'Unto us a child is born, unto us a son is given.'** There is no repetition here. The careful student knows that the Spirit does no waste words.

'A child is born' — a man-child made of a woman, who lay nine months in the womb and came forth as all children are born, bone of our bone and flesh of our flesh. Jesus Christ, the man, was born of a woman, just as all men come into the world.

'A son is given.' This son was not just born, but given, sent from heaven. He was 'made of the seed of David according to the flesh; and declared to be the Son of God with power' (Rom. 1:3-4).

When the angel announced to Joseph the coming of Christ in the flesh, he quoted Isaiah 7:14, saying, 'A virgin shall be with child, and shall bring forth a son, and shall call his name Emmanuel ... God with us' (Matt. 1:23). The virgin birth is not simply a matter for argument or amazement, but of necessity. Jesus Christ is not only man and called the Son of Man, but he is God and the Son of God. The Son of God can have no human father, but is conceived by the Holy Ghost. If he were the seed of man and not the seed of woman, he would be born in sin, but he is 'holy, harmless, undefiled, separate from sinners' (Heb. 7:26).

Is it true that God became a man? If it is true, then we have a righteousness, a redeemer, a mediator and a hope of eternal glory. If it is not true, if there is no man in glory called Jesus Christ, then no other man will ever be in glory and we stand alone before God's throne with no mediator (1 Tim. 2:5).

2. **'The government shall be upon his shoulder'** — the government, not only of the universe and the world in general, but of the kingdom of God in particular.

> All things in heaven and earth were made by him, for him and are held together by him (Col. 1:16-17).
>
> He has all authority in heaven and earth (Matt. 28:18) and all authority over all flesh (John 17:2).
>
> He reigns as king and surety over the kingdom of God. This government is delegated to him from the Father (1 Cor. 15:24-28).
>
> He is head of the church, has all pre-eminence (Col. 1:18-19) and a name that is above every name (Phil. 2:9-11).

3. **'His name shall be called Wonderful.'** We carelessly call many things wonderful that are unworthy of such distinction. He alone is wonderful. He is wonderful in his eternality (Prov. 8:24-

31); wonderful in his person — the God-man; wonderful in his everlasting, infinite and unchanging love; wonderful in his perfect, holy life; wonderful in his substitutionary death; wonderful in his resurrection, ascension and exaltation at the right hand of God (Heb. 1:1-4).

4. **'Counsellor.'** The world is full of people who want to be counsellors and advisers, but there is only one counsellor — Jesus Christ. Would you know God? Christ reveals him! Would you know the will, way and purpose of God? They are all found in Christ! He is both the wisdom and the power of God (1 Cor. 1:30). Someone asked Mr Spurgeon, 'What is the best body of divinity?' He replied, 'There is but one body of divinity — Christ Jesus' (Col. 2:9-10). Religious people say, 'Are you in trouble? Do you need the Lord? Then call us.' Don't do it! Call on Christ; he is the Counsellor!

5. **'The mighty God.'** The disciples said, 'Show us the Father.' Christ replied, 'He that hath seen me hath seen the Father' (John 14:8,9). 'I and my Father are one' (John 10:30). Jesus Christ is God (Acts 20:28; 2 Cor. 5:19; Heb. 1:8). Every attribute of deity is found in him — omnipotence, omniscience, omnipresence. The disciples asked, 'What manner of man is this, that even the winds and the sea obey him?' (Matt. 8:27; Mark 4:41). He is the mighty God!

6. **'The everlasting Father.'** No man can explain the Trinity; we can only believe. Our God is one God, yet three persons — Father, Son and Holy Spirit (1 John 5:7). He that has the Son hath the Father (2 John 9; 1 John 2:23). When Moses asked God, 'What is thy name?' the Lord replied, 'I AM THAT I AM.' On how many occasions did our Lord Jesus use these words, 'I am'? (John 8:58).

7. **'The Prince of Peace.'** He is the author of peace between God and sinners (Rom. 5:1; Col. 1:20). He is our peace of heart and conscience (John 14:27). He brings to us everlasting peace. for his government, his peace and his kingdom are established on principles of judgement and justice (Isa. 9:7). This is no temporary peace, for Jesus Christ, the God-man, effectually, sufficiently and once for all honoured God's law and satisfied justice for all who believe (2 Cor. 5:21; 1 Peter 3:18; Acts 13:38-39).

29. The day of divine visitation

Isaiah 12:1-6

This chapter contains a song of praise and thanksgiving for redemption and salvation in Christ Jesus. This is strictly 'family fare' and cannot be appreciated, understood, or sung by any but the redeemed of the Lord.

v.1. **'And in that day.'** This is a phrase used repeatedly by Isaiah to indicate a particular time of divine visitation. It may not be a twenty-four hour day, but rather a time when the Lord is pleased to reveal to his elect his grace and mercy in Christ.

1. It is a day of conviction (Isa. 2:10-11); for judgement precedes justification, emptying precedes filling, repentance precedes comfort.
2. It is a day of revelation (Isa. 25:8-9) when, like Simeon of old, the believer cries, 'I have seen thy salvation!'
3. It is a day of assurance (Isa. 26:1-4), when his rest, peace and joy settle upon the heart and mind, and we are enabled to trust him with complete confidence.

'I will praise thee: though thou wast angry with me, thine anger is turned away, and thou comfortedst me.' The Lord's anger towards his elect is difficult to explain in the light of the fact that he has loved us 'with an everlasting love' (Jer. 31:3), and he declared, 'Jacob have I loved', before Jacob was born (Rom. 9:13). But the Scriptures say, 'We ... were by nature children of wrath, even as others' (Eph. 2:3-4), and 'At that time, [we Gentiles] were without Christ ... and without God' (Eph. 2:12). Whatever it means, we know that in Christ Jesus his anger and wrath are turned away (Rom. 8:31-33,38-39). 'God was in Christ, reconciling [us] unto himself' (2 Cor. 5:19), and we are comforted by his promises, by his love shed abroad in our hearts and by his indwelling Spirit (John 14:16-18; 16:13-14).

v.2. **'Behold, God is my salvation.'** This may read, 'God is my Saviour.' Christ, who is God, is my Saviour (John 1:1,14). He is a just God and a Saviour (Isa. 45:21). He was appointed by the Father, provided in the covenant, promised in the Word, sent in the fulness of time and became the author of my salvation by his obedience, death and exaltation (Acts 13:38-39; 1 Peter 3:18).

'I will trust, and not be afraid: for the Lord Jehovah is my strength and my song.' I will trust him for all things needed and required — wisdom, righteousness, sanctification and redemption (1 Cor. 1:30). I will rest confidently in him and trust that in him I am secure from all wrath and condemnation (Rom. 8:1,33-34). I will not be afraid of sin, Satan, death, hell, or the wrath to come (Isa. 26:3-4).

'He also is become my salvation.' In the light of our weakness, failure and flesh, how can we have such confidence and assurance of our security and acceptance before God? Because he is our salvation! He is our strength! He is our song! God set him forth to be a mercy-seat; God laid on him our iniquities; God made us accepted in the Beloved. 'How shall he not with him also freely give us all things', accomplished by our Redeemer-God? (Rom. 8:32). It would be nothing short of blasphemy to reckon that God would renege on his promises to Christ and his church (Isa. 46:9-11; Rom. 11:29).

v.3. **'Therefore with joy shall ye draw water out of the wells of salvation.'** The Father is called 'the fountain of living waters' (Jer. 2:13). The Lord Jesus is the giver of living water (John 4:10,14). The Holy Spirit is the source of 'rivers of living water' (John 7:38-39). These are the wells of salvation, and from them with joy we draw water (grace) for every need. Our needs go beyond a once-for-all justification and acceptance; our needs are daily needs. He taught us to pray, 'Give us this day our daily bread,' which is not only food for the body, but comfort, faith, joy, peace, strength and love. I must always remain at the fountain, 'drawing water' for my thirsty soul.

v.4. **'And in that day shall ye say...'** If there has indeed been for you a day of divine visitation, of conviction, of revelation, of mercy, then shall you say:

1. **'Praise the Lord,'** for mercy to this chief of sinners, for all spiritual blessings in Christ Jesus (Eph. 1:3-7).

2. **'Call upon his name,'** which takes in the whole of worship. To worship God is to call upon his name. Whether in faith for mercy, in prayer, in thanksgiving, in trial, or in a daily walk, we constantly 'call upon his name'.

3. **'Declare his doings among the people'** — not only his works of creation, of providence and miracles, but especially his doing and dying to redeem a people. 'I have finished the work which thou gavest me to do' (John 17:4). That work of redemption is the 'doings' that we especially declare.

4. **'Make mention that his name is exalted'** (Phil. 2:5-11).

There's none other name given among men,
There's none can with him compare;
All others are marred,
By sin they are scarred;
He's fairer than all the fair.

v.5. **'Sing unto the Lord; for he hath done excellent things.'** Sing psalms, hymns and spiritual songs, vocally and together, as gospel churches, to the glory of God. Let him be the subject of our songs, for he has done great things for us and in us and he will yet glorify the riches of his grace to us! He is worthy to be praised by all his creatures (Ps. 150).

v.6. **'Cry out and shout,'** all you who are in Zion (his church), **'for great is the Holy One of Israel in the midst of thee.'** Christ Jesus is the Holy One of Israel, the head of the church, and he has promised and grants his presence to his church; wherefore, he is worthy of our praise — for his greatness, for his mercy and for his grace.

30. The believer's comfort

Isaiah 40:1-9

v.1. **'Comfort ye, comfort ye my people, saith your God.'**

Who speaks? It is the Lord God of hosts. Do we have ears to hear what the Lord says?

To whom does he speak? He speaks to his prophets, preachers, pastors, teachers — all who are bondservants of the Lord.

What is his commandment? 'Comfort ye my people.' There is a time to rebuke, reprove and correct and there is a time for examination, but the command here is to comfort!

Who are his people? We cannot comfort where God has not converted. We cannot cry 'peace' when there is no peace. We cannot give false assurance to rebels. Who are his people? They are a chosen people, a called people, a redeemed people and a believing people.

Why do they need comfort? They are saved sinners who are conscious of their infirmities; they are a tried people, who have troubles in the flesh; they are a persecuted people, who are hated by the world.

v.2. What shall I say to his people to comfort them? What is the believer's source of greatest comfort? It is the good news of the gospel!

'Cry unto her, that her warfare is accomplished.' The battle is over and 'Thanks be to God, which giveth us the victory through our Lord Jesus Christ' (1 Cor. 15:55-58). All of our enemies have been engaged by our Captain, and they are conquered and shall soon be under our feet, as they are now under his: sin (Heb. 10:17-18), self (Gal. 2:20), Satan (John 14:30; 16:11), the world (John 16:33) and death (John 11:25-26).

'Her iniquity is pardoned.' All of our sins (past, present and future) are blotted out, cleansed, atoned for and remembered no more. The redeemed have no sins. 'With his spotless garments on, they are as holy as God's Son.'

'Double for all her sins.' This denotes the sufficiency of his blood and the complete satisfaction made by Christ for all our sins. Not that more was required than was due; but his offering, being infinite, fully answers more than double what can be demanded. 'Where sin did overflow, grace did much more overflow.'

vv.3-5. John the Baptist is the voice crying in the wilderness of Judea. There is a threefold effect of his office: the humiliation of some, the exaltation of others and the revelation of the glory of Christ Jesus.

'Prepare ye the way of the Lord.' The Messiah comes and John calls upon men to repent, to lay aside all thoughts and ways contrary to his gospel and kingdom and to embrace him when he comes.

'Every valley shall be exalted.' When Messiah comes, all who are depressed and bowed down with the guilt of sin, labouring and heavy laden, low and humble in their own eyes, shall be raised up and comforted.

'Every mountain and hill shall be made low.' The proud and haughty shall be brought down. Those who are elated with themselves and their own righteousness shall be humbled.

'The crooked shall be made straight, and the rough places plain.' Could this be that those types, patterns and pictures of the Old Testament should become clear in Christ, and prophecies, not so well understood, would be now plain and easy? (Luke 24:27,44-45).

'And the glory of the Lord shall be revealed.' Christ himself, who is the brightness of the Father's glory (Heb. 1:1-3), reveals his redemptive glory (Exod. 33:18-19), which is his chief glory.

'All flesh shall see it' — not the Jews only, but Gentiles also, and not with bodily eyes, but with the eyes of their understanding, even the salvation of the Lord and his glory displayed in it. The everlasting gospel is called the gospel of his glory (1 Tim. 1:11; 1 Cor. 1:26-31).

vv.6-9. I prefer to look at these verses together, for I see the twofold, actually, the threefold, message of evangelism. Here is a command, **'Cry!'** and a question, **'What shall I cry?'** What shall I preach? What is the message men need to hear?

'**All flesh is grass, and all the goodliness thereof**', all its glory and comeliness, '**is as the flower of the field.**' All flesh (young and old, Jew and Gentile, religious and profane) is like worthless, withering grass. We are born spiritually dead and worthless; nothing we can do in life improves the condition, and the death of the flesh only confirms its corrupt condition. In the flesh 'dwelleth no good thing' (Rom. 7:18), and in the flesh no man can please God (Rom. 8:8). This must be preached in order to humble the pride of men and to show the necessity of divine power in regeneration (John 3:5-7). Not only is all flesh grass, but even man's so-called righteousness (that which is comely and commendable compared to others) is as worthless as a fading flower (Isa. 64:6). Man at his best state is altogether vanity. We find this out when '**the spirit of the Lord bloweth upon it**', for he makes us to know the truth about ourselves in the light of God's holiness (Isa. 6:5; Job 42:5-6).

'**The word of our God shall stand for ever**' (v.8). This may be applied to the recorded Word of our God, which is sure and certain, for ever settled in heaven and always fulfilled, or rather, Christ the Word, who stands for ever in his office, in the efficacy of his blood, in the fulness of his grace and in the glory of his exaltation (Col. 1:16-18).

'**Behold your God!**' (v.9). Get up on a high mountain, lift up your voice, be not afraid, and say unto the people, 'Behold your God!' John Gill said it best: 'Behold your God! That Divine person is come that was promised, prophesied and expected; even Emmanuel, God with us, God in our nature, God manifest in the flesh, God your Saviour; and who, being God, truly God, is able to save to the uttermost. Look to Him with an eye of faith and be saved. Behold your God! Behold the Son of God, the Lamb of God, who has borne our sins and taken them away. Behold Him now, as your King and your God, on the throne, made and declared Christ and Lord, crowned with glory and honour, on the same throne with His heavenly Father, having all power in heaven and earth, and let the echo of your faith be, "My Lord and my God."'

31. The Messiah

Isaiah 42:1-21

This is one of the many places in the book of Isaiah which absolutely cannot be applied to anyone but the Messiah. It is evident that the prophet speaks of the Christ, for our Lord Jesus confirmed it in Matthew 12:14-21. Time and space will not permit us to comment on every word, so we shall try to touch the high points.

v.1. His condescension. **'Behold my servant'** — the Messiah, who was with God, who is God and who 'thought it not robbery to be equal with God: but made himself of no reputation, and took upon him the form of a servant' (Phil. 2:6-8). He is the servant, not of angels and men, but of the divine Father, who chose him, called him and sent him to accomplish the redemption of his people.

'Whom I uphold', strengthen and help, as man and mediator, so that he did not sink under the weight of the sins of his people and the wrath of God.

'Mine elect':

1. God chose men and not angels (Heb. 2:16).
2. Christ is chosen, and we were chosen in him (Eph. 1:3-4).
3. God delights in, and is well pleased with him, and with us as we are considered in him (Eph. 1:6-7).
4. God puts his Spirit upon him, not as a divine person, but as a man for the work he would do (John 3:34-36).
5. By himself he shall bring forth righteousness, truth and justice to the nations.

vv.2-3. His humility and tenderness. Earthly kings and rulers cry out in defence of their programmes, strive with others, lift up their standards and campaign in the streets. They have no use for the weak and weary, nor the frail and the faint, and their means are justified by their goals. But our Messiah is meek and lowly in heart, a tender plant, a man of sorrows, who opens not his mouth. He does not strive, or contend to no profit. His kingdom is not of this world, so he does not boast and try to rally support for himself in the streets. His kingdom is a spiritual kingdom; his enemies are principalities and powers, rulers of darkness who are conquered and defeated by himself alone; his people are made willing in the day of his power by his Spirit and his gospel call. He came, by his identification with us, his obedience and death, to save sinners, weak and unworthy, frail and fainting; so he does not break the bruised, weak reed, but strengthens it! He does not quench the flickering lamp, but gives it oil to burn brighter. The bruised reed and the flickering, dimly burning lamp are his weak and frail people who are not cast off, but comforted and cared for tenderly. His work is judgement and justice. The courts of heaven shall receive his people, for he justifies them on the basis of truth and righteousness (Rom. 3:25-26).

v.4. His success. **'He shall not fail nor be discouraged.'** What the Father purposed, the Son purchased and the Spirit applied. How can it even be imagined that our God should fail to accomplish his redemptive will and work? (Isa. 46:9-11; 53:10-11; John 6:37-39).

'Till he have set judgement in the earth.' He fully satisfied the justice of God for the sins of his people, settled and sent his gospel to call out his people and sat down at the right hand of majesty till all that he purposed and performed shall be accomplished. **'The isles'** (islands, distant countries and all nations) in hope wait for his word of grace, for he shall have a people from them all (Ps. 110:1-3).

vv.5-7. His assignment. How often did our Lord Jesus refer to 'the work which thou gavest me to do'! (John 4:34; 9:4; 17:4).

1. The greatness of our God, who called and sent the Messiah, is set forth. He has the power, greatness and authority to do what he will.

2. **'I ... have called'** and sent the Messiah **'in righteousness'**, or in a righteous manner consistent with God's perfections (Ps. 85:10-13). Christ came, a holy person (Heb. 7:25-26), and fully obeyed God's law (Rom. 5:19).

3. Christ was held, kept, sustained and given to us as the surety, mediator, sum and substance of God's everlasting covenant of grace (Heb. 13:20-21). All the blessings and promises of the covenant are in him, by him and given through him (Heb. 10:14-18).

4. He came **'to open the blind eyes'** — spiritually blind — to enable them by his gospel to see the sinfulness of sin, their need of a Saviour and who he is! He came to set the prisoners free — prisoners of sin, shut up to unbelief and under the judgement of the broken law, in the darkness of spiritual death and ignorance (Luke 4:17-18). 'If the Son ... shall make you free, ye shall be free indeed' (John 8:36).

vv.8-9. His name and knowledge. **'I am Jehovah.'** His name expresses his eternality, his immutability, his redemptive character. It is the name by which he made himself known to Israel of old, as 'a just God and a Saviour' (Isa. 45:21). His name expresses his character and his redemptive glory (Exod. 33:18-19), which he will not give to another. Men who truly believe his name, call upon his name and glorify his name will be saved (Rom. 10:13-14). He declares the former things and the new things before they come to pass (Isa. 46:10).

vv.10-12. His praise. These verses are summed up briefly in one phrase: **'Let them give glory unto the Lord, and declare his praise'** (see Ps. 150).

vv.13-15. His victory over his enemies. The Lord, for many ages, has permitted Satan, idolaters and rebels to go to and fro. He will one day roar, destroy and devour them at once. The last enemy, death, will one day be destroyed and righteousness will reign universally.

vv.16-21. His redemptive glory. Verses 16-18 are spoken of the Gentiles, who will be made to see and hear what they have never seen and heard, and verses 19-20 refer to the Jews, who are called the servants and messengers of God and who claim to see and be perfect. But there is none so blind and deaf as those who think they see and hear but do not! But **'the Lord is well pleased'** (v.21) with the obedience and righteousness of the Lord Jesus, who in life and

death magnified God's law and made it honourable. There is
nothing so important to any who would know God as to be taught by
God's Spirit three things:

1. The holiness of our God;
2. The sinfulness and inability of our flesh;
3. The righteousness of God effectually and sufficiently
displayed in, and wrought out by, our Lord Jesus (2 Cor. 5:21;
Rom. 10:1-4).

32. A just God and a Saviour

Isaiah 45:16-25

This chapter contains prophecies concerning Cyrus (the deliverer of the Jews from captivity) and the great things God would do for him and by him (vv.1-3). The reasons God would do these things were for the sake of Israel and that he might be known to be the only true God, who is the maker and owner of all things (vv.4-7). A declaration is made of the Messiah as the author of salvation and righteousness (v.8) and the contention and murmuring of the Jews about the Messiah, Son of Man (vv.9-10). Christ is the antitype of Cyrus, and the Lord says, 'Ask of me, and expect great things to be done by me, through the Messiah whom I have raised up in righteousness. He shall build my city' (vv.11-13). The conversion of the Gentiles is prophesied, who will come over to the church, subdued and conquered by the grace of God, saying, 'God,' the only God, 'is in thee' (v.14). God is sovereign in mercy and will reveal himself as Saviour when and to whom he will (v.15). But the makers of idols and worshippers of false gods shall be confounded and ashamed for ever (v.16).

v.17. **'But Israel shall be saved in the Lord.'** The word 'Israel' is used in the Bible over 2,500 times. Most of the time it refers to *the nation* of Israel, the typical people. But here and in many other places it refers to *spiritual* Israel — the true people of God among all nations. True Israel are the sons of Abraham in Christ, the seed (Rom. 4:16; Gal. 3:7,16,29). 'He is not a Jew [Israel] which is one outwardly' (Rom. 2:28-29; 9:7-8). All who are given to Christ, all for whom he died, who are called to repentance and faith, are Israel and shall be saved **'with an everlasting salvation'** (Mal. 3:6; Rom. 11:29; John 6:37-39). They shall never be ashamed or put to shame; they are saved for ever!

v.18. This is no idle promise! God's creation is not in vain. He created the heavens and the earth; and out of all of it will come his new heaven and new earth, which he formed to be inhabited by a people conformed to the image of Christ (Rom. 8:19-23,29-30). The end of all things was already decreed and determined by our God before one stone was laid in the earth's foundations (Isa. 46:9-11; Eph. 1:3-6).

v.19. This covenant of grace and plan of redemption is no secret plan! God said, 'I did not whisper the way of life in secret; I did not hide it in a dark place, nor did I say in vain to the sons of Jacob, "Seek ye the Lord."' God, the Lord, speaks in righteousness and justice to all the earth. He has made known his law, his righteousness and holiness and his mercy to sinners by his grace through the one great mediator, high priest and atonement, which enables him to be both just and justifier (Rom. 3:19-26). The Scriptures (translated into 2,000 languages) are clear to all who read, but 'Ye will not come to [Christ]' (John 5:39-40).

v.20. Men who turn from the Almighty God to their own gods and ways of salvation have no knowledge, for they pray to, and preach about, an impotent god who cannot save. The god of men cannot do his will, but must wait upon the will of the creature. The living God cannot lie and can do nothing contrary to his nature, but he can save sinners, for in his infinite wisdom and power he has provided in Christ a righteousness which enables him to be 'a just God and a Saviour' (v.21; Rom. 10:1-4).

v.21. He has declared this glorious salvation from ancient times, from before the foundation of the world (Eph. 1:3-4; 2 Thess. 2:13; Matt. 25:34; 1 Peter 1:20; Rev. 13:8). Who can do this? Who alone can declare the end from the beginning? Only the sovereign, almighty, omnipotent God, and there is none beside him. But here is a key — a truth to be learned: he is **'a just God and a Saviour'**. In saving sinners God cannot, will not and does not compromise his holiness. That is why Christ, the God-man, must come, must obey the law, must die on the cross — to enable God to be holy as well as merciful (Rom. 3:25-26; 2 Cor. 5:21; Rom. 1:16-17).

v.22. Then to whom should we look if we would be saved? To whom *must* we look if we would be saved? To him!

The word is **'look'**, not 'labour' or 'serve'. These things are the results of salvation, but salvation and eternal life are the gift of God through the person and work of Christ. Only believe and live! (John 3:14-16,36; Acts 13:38-39).

'All the ends of the earth.' All men died in Adam, all men are under the curse of sin and all men (Jew or Gentile) will look to Christ and be saved or they will perish (John 14:6; Acts 4:11-12).

v.23. **'I have sworn by myself.'** Christ, being the true God, can swear by no greater (Heb. 6:13). This shows that what follows is of the greatest importance.

'The word is gone out of my mouth in righteousness,' concerning how men are to be saved, in a manner agreeable to truth and justice, **'and shall not return'**, or be changed. Unto Christ Jesus every knee shall bow and every tongue confess that he is Lord (Phil. 2:9-11). Men will repent, believe and own Christ to be their Lord now and be saved (Rom. 10:9-10), or they will, in the Day of Judgement, confess it in their utter damnation.

v.24. This is the confession of all believers: 'In the Lord Jesus Christ we have righteousness, acceptance and strength.' We came to him and, in coming to him, we came to God (1 Peter 3:18). We were at one time **'incensed against him'** and are ashamed of our unbelief, and those who continue to reject him **'shall be ashamed'** eternally.

v.25. All of spiritual Israel, whether Jew or Gentile, given to Christ, represented by Christ, redeemed by Christ and interceded for by Christ, will be justified in him and will glory in him — not in themselves, but in him who is made unto us all we need (1 Cor. 1:30-31).

33. The Redeemer describes himself

Isaiah 50:1-11

All Scriptures declare and reveal the person and work of Christ Jesus, our Redeemer (Acts 10:43). He is the 'key of knowledge' denied by the Pharisees and lawyers (Luke 11:52). When Paul wrote, 'He died, was buried and rose again according to the Scriptures,' he was referring to the Old Testament Scriptures, such as those before us (1 Cor. 15:3).

v.1. **'Where is the bill of your mother's divorcement?'** When a man divorced his wife, he was required to give her a paper stating that he had officially divorced her. Our Lord says, 'You have no such bill; I did not forsake you.'

'Which of my creditors is it to whom I have sold you?' When a man was so heavily in debt that he could not pay, he would sell his children into slavery to satisfy his debts. The Lord owes no one; he has no creditors.

The truth of the matter is: **'For your iniquities have ye sold yourselves, and for your transgressions'** you are separated from God. Man's ruin, spiritual death and slavery lie at his own door. 'Your iniquities have separated between you and your God' (Isa. 59:1-2).

vv.2-3. **'Wherefore, when I came, was there no man?'** 'He was in the world ... and the world knew him not. He came unto his own, and his own received him not' (John 1:10-11; Isa. 53:1-3).

'When I called, was there none to answer?' He called to peace, rest and to the marriage feast, and they made light of it. He stretched out his hand, and no man regarded (Prov. 1:24-28). Sinners are not to be pitied, but rather to be blamed, for our condemnation is our own fault.

God is able to save; he is able to redeem all who call upon him. He has power to deliver; nothing is too hard for our God.

1. He dried up the sea for Israel to cross over.
2. He made the River Jordan a wilderness.
3. He clothed the heavens with blackness (Exod. 10:21).
4. He made sackcloth to cover the sun (Rev. 6:12).

Preachers today may make man to be more than he is and God to be less than he is, but when our God describes himself, he declares his majesty, power and total sovereignty (Rom. 9:15-16). The Bible knows nothing of an impotent God, nor a doormat named Jesus. He declares, 'I have spoken it, I will ... bring it to pass; I have purposed it, I will ... do it.' 'My counsel shall stand, and I will do all my pleasure' (Isa. 46:9-11; Rom. 8:29-31).

v.4. The Lord describes his *prophetic office.* You are no doubt familiar with the fact that our Lord has a threefold office. He is the *King*, typified by David. As King he reigns over all by decree, by design and by the fact that he died that he might be Lord. He is the *Priest* for ever after the order of Melchisedek (Heb. 7:17-25) and he is that *Prophet* spoken of by Moses (Deut. 18:18-19). 'This is my beloved Son ... hear ye him' (Matt. 17:5; Heb. 1:1-2). 'He that hath seen me hath seen the Father ... the words that I speak unto you I speak not of myself: but the Father that dwelleth in me, he doeth the works' (John 14:9-10). 'No man ... knoweth ... the Father, save the Son, and he to whomsoever the Son will reveal him' (Matt. 11:27; Luke 11:22; John 17:6-8). Our Prophet reveals and manifests the Father's will, word and work.

v.5. The Redeemer declares his *submission* as the messenger of the covenant and the Father's servant (Isa. 42:1). He is the God-man and servant who was willing to do all that was required to redeem the elect. 'The Lord has digged, or bored, my ear.' This comes from the Scripture in Exodus 21:1-6, where the slave who has served his time and is free to go chooses, out of love for his master, to remain as a willing, loving bondslave and has his ear bored before the judges. 'No man taketh [my life] from me; I lay it down of myself', willingly, out of love for the Father's will and love for his people (John 10:18).

v.6. The Redeemer describes himself as the *Suffering Servant*. 'He opened not his mouth' against the witnesses, the charges, nor those who abused him (Isa. 53:7). He gave his back to the smiters (Matt. 27:26) and his face to those who spit upon him and pulled out his beard (Matt. 26:67). The suffering and death of our Redeemer was no accident, nor an unexpected tragedy. It was decreed by the Father (Acts 2:23; 4:27-28), prophesied in Scripture (Isa. 53:4-6; Acts 13:29) and fulfilled by the Son — willingly.

vv.7-9. The Redeemer describes the *success of his work.*

'The Lord God will help me.' This is no contradiction of the deity of Christ, nor any sign of weakness in him, but he was a man, with the weaknesses and limitations of flesh, and needed the strength and power of his God to effect the greatness of the work of our redemption (Luke 22:42-43).

'Therefore shall I not be confounded ... and I know that I shall not be ashamed,' neither of his ministry (which was with power and authority in truth), nor of his obedience (which was perfect and pleasing to the Father), nor of his sufferings (for the sake of his people), nor of his work of redemption (which was effectual) (John 17:4-5).

'Therefore have I set my face like a flint' (cf. Luke 9:51), for **'He is near that justifieth me.'** The Father designed and decreed his death and sent him into the world. The Father was near him in his whole state of humiliation and justified him from all the false charges brought against him and from the sins of his people laid upon him, as evidenced by his resurrection (Acts 13:29-30; 17:31).

'Who will contend with me? ... Who is he that shall condemn me?' Not Satan, nor the law, nor the justice of God. Satan came and found nothing in him, and he honoured the law and satisfied justice.

vv.10-11. The Lord sets forth two classes of people:

1. Those who fear the Lord and have been given ears to hear the voice of Christ and see the glory of God in the face of Christ. They know they are in the darkness of sin and have no light; therefore they look to Christ, trust him for all truth and righteousness and stay upon their God. These shall never be ashamed.

2. But there are those who will not come to him, but rather depend upon their own works and righteousness. They **'kindle a fire'** and walk in the light of their own fire. These shall lie down in death and eternal sorrow and have judgement at God's hand.

34. Our confession of faith

Isaiah 53

Someone asked an old minister of the gospel, 'Is your creed in print?' He replied, 'Yes, you will find it all in Isaiah, chapter 53.' Here is the gospel of God's grace in one chapter.

v.1. **'Our report'** is our message of the love, mercy and grace of God in Christ Jesus. It is the testimony of God concerning Jesus Christ (Rom. 1:1-4). There has never lived a prophet who did not mourn the fact that men would not believe the good news of grace.

'The arm of the Lord' is Christ Jesus, the wisdom and power of God, for the gospel of Christ is the power of God unto salvation (Rom. 1:16). Natural men do not see, hear, or understand how God can be both just and justifier, righteous and yet merciful to sinners through the obedience and death of Christ, the substitute (1 Cor. 2:8-14). He must be revealed to the heart by the Holy Spirit.

v.2. **'A tender plant'** signifies his lowly entrance into the world. He came, not full grown in the pomp and glory of men, but as a tiny, frail, helpless infant, born of a woman (Gal. 4:4-5).

'A root out of a dry ground' reveals the condition of David's house and the nation of Israel at this time. There was nothing left of the glory of David's kingdom, only dry ground, its king an unlikely son of a carpenter (John 6:42).

'No form nor comeliness ... no beauty.' In sending our Redeemer into the world, the Lord God rejected and refused all fleshly, human attraction. Anything that would attract the eye of the flesh or support of the natural mind was refused. 'My kingdom is not of this world' (John 18:36; 1:10-11).

v.3. **'Despised and rejected of men.'** Because of the lowliness of his birth, the poverty of his parents, his home town and vocation, his lack of formal education, the people with whom he associated, his personal habits, the doctrine he preached, his claim to be one with the Father and his condemnation of their tradition, everybody who was anybody turned from him, **'esteemed him not'** and despised him.

'A man of sorrows, and acquainted with grief.' From the cradle to the grave, two words can sum up his pilgrimage through this world: 'Jesus wept' (John 11:35; Lam. 1:12).

v.4. **'He hath borne our griefs, and carried our sorrows.'** The grief and sorrows, spiritual infirmities and sicknesses (Matt. 8:17), which he bore were not his own but ours. He had no sin, knew no sin and did no sin. He was our substitute and representative.

'Stricken, smitten of God, and afflicted.' The wrath of God and the sword of God's justice were sharpened to pierce him because he bore our sins and stood in our place. Though he had no sin, he stood before the justice of God as the world's greatest sinner, for on him were laid all the sins of all the elect of all ages.

v.5. If you would learn the gospel, then learn the meaning of these two words: 'substitution' and 'satisfaction'.

'He was wounded for our transgressions.' He was literally our substitute before the law and justice of God. In our place, in our stead, bearing our transgressions and all of our iniquities, he took upon himself all that justice could inflict.

He made full satisfaction, for by **'his stripes we are healed'**. God is reconciled, the debt is paid, justice is satisfied. He fully reconciled us to God by his obedience and his death (2 Cor. 5:19-21). The heart of the sinner was not changed towards God in the sufferings of Christ (that is accomplished later by the Holy Spirit and the Word), but the wrath of God was removed towards the sinner. Reconciliation is the work of God in Christ towards himself (Rom. 3:24-26).

v.6. The prophet is careful not to say 'they' or 'them,' but **'we'** — **'all we like sheep'** and **'the iniquity of us all'**! Read verses 4-6 and put your name in every place where you read **'our'** and **'we'**. Someone wrote,

My sins, my sins, my Saviour,
How sad on thee they fall;
When I see them in thy death,
I tenfold own them all.

My sins, my sins, my Saviour,
Their guilt I never knew;
Till I saw them at the cross,
The Lord of hosts they slew.

v.7. **'He opened not his mouth.'** He was a willing Redeemer. 'No man takes my life; I lay it down.' He was brought as a lamb to the altar, as a sheep to be shorn of all dignity, comfort, honour and even his life. 'Yet he opened not his mouth,' not against his people, his Father, his enemies, or justice. He was willing to die for his sheep (John 10:14-18).

v.8. His life was taken away in a violent manner, under a pretence of justice. Wrong charges were brought against him; false witnesses lied.
    'He was cut off out of the land of the living.' Who shall declare the wickedness of men? But **'For the transgression of [his] people was he stricken'** (1 Peter 3:18).

v.9. **'He made his grave with the wicked,'** signifies that he was assigned to die between two thieves.
    'And with the rich in his death,' denotes the fact that he was laid in the borrowed tomb of a rich man. Such vile and wicked treatment was accorded him, although he had done no violence and knew no sin.

v.10. **'It pleased the Lord to bruise him.'** This is a key verse. The Lord bruised him, the Lord put him to grief and the Lord made his soul an offering for sin. The Father not only permitted him to suffer as our substitute and sin-offering, he purposed it, predestinated it and willed him to die (Acts 2:22-23; 4:26-28).
    His soul-suffering will make **'an offering'**, an atonement for our sins and **'He shall see his seed'** (every son, sheep and elect person is seen, known and loved by Christ).

'**He shall prolong his days**' (he lives for ever, and so shall they), and '**The pleasure,**' purpose, and will of the Father '**shall prosper,**' be accomplished, fulfilled, '**in his hands**' (John 3:35; Eph. 1:3-14).

v.11. Our Lord did not suffer in vain. He is '**satisfied**', even seated, having finished his work! All for whom he suffered are justified, for he bore their iniquities (Rom. 8:29-32).

> Payment God's justice cannot twice demand,
> First at my bleeding Surety's hand,
> And then again at mine.

v.12. He is exalted above all exaltation (Phil. 2:9-11), and '**He shall divide the spoil with the strong**' because:

1. '**He hath poured out his soul unto death**' — satisfaction.
2. '**He was numbered with the transgressors**' — representation..
3. '**He bare the sin of many**' — substitution.
4. '**He ... made intercession for the transgressors**' — mediation.

35. 'Seek ye the Lord'

Isaiah 55

Isaiah 53 sets forth the *gospel provided* through the suffering Saviour. Isaiah 54 sets forth the *gospel promises* that are sure and certain (vv.10,16-17). Isaiah 55 sets forth the *gospel proclaimed* to the needy. The mercies of God in Christ are a proclamation to all men (Mark 16:15) and an effectual call to his sheep (John 10: 27-29).

v.1. **'Ho, every one that thirsteth,'** not in a natural sense as the woman at the well first thought, but everyone whose soul thirsts for fellowship with God (for mercy, forgiveness and life) is called to the fountain of life.

'**Come ... to the waters.'** Come to the water of life that cleanses and refreshes, to the wine that makes the heart glad and to the milk which gives life and health. It is free to those who are poor and have nothing to pay; it has already been paid for by the blood of Christ (Rom. 3:24).

v.2. Why do men spend time, energy and strength in pursuing a false religion which is not the bread of life and can never satisfy? Salvation by works is not bread; it is chaff. It is not nourishing; it is harmful. It will not satisfy, only condemn! 'Listen to me,' says the Lord, and feed upon Christ, and your soul will rest and delight itself in his fulness (Col. 2:9-10).

v.3. Here are two precepts and two promises.

The precepts:

1. **'Incline your ear.'** Is this asking too much of beggars, of guilty sinners? The body is fed through the mouth, and the

soul is fed through the ear. Your can hear the error of the world and poison your soul, or you can hear the precious Word of God and live. 'He that hath ears to hear, let him hear.'

2. **'Come unto me'** (Isa. 1:18; Matt. 11:28; John 7:37-38). Don't turn to religion, to law, or to men. 'Come to me.'

The promises:

1. **'And your soul shall live.'** There is power and life in the gospel (Rom.1:16; James 1:18). All that God has for sinners is in Christ. Those spiritual blessings are ours through a union with Christ; that union with Christ comes by faith; faith comes by hearing the word of truth (Eph. 1:13-14).

2. **'I will make an everlasting covenant with you, even the sure mercies of David.'** Peter calls these 'precious promises'. This is the everlasting covenant which David (on his dying bed) called 'all my salvation, and all my desire' (2 Sam. 23:5). Here are five of those sure mercies of David:

'I ... will be their God, and they shall be my people' (Jer. 31:33).

'They shall all know me' (Jer. 31:34).

'I will forgive their iniquity, and I will remember their sin no more' (Jer. 31:34).

'I will give them one heart, and one way' (Jer. 32:39).

'I will not turn away from them ... [and] they shall not depart from me' (Jer. 32:40).

v.4. This everlasting covenant is made with our surety, that Great Shepherd of the sheep, Christ Jesus (Heb. 13:20). The Lord has given him for a witness, for he is that Prophet who manifests and reveals the Father (Deut. 18:18-19). He is a leader, for he is our great High Priest after the order of Melchizedek; he is our Shepherd, who leads us in the paths of righteousness, and he is commander, or King of kings!

v.5. We do not look to, or follow, him in vain, for he will not fail (Isa. 42:1-4). He will call and save the Gentiles, who will willingly run to him because of the power of God (Ps. 110:3). All that Christ is, does and will do for his people will be for the glory of God (John 17:1-4; 1 Cor. 15:27-28; Eph. 1:6,12,14).

v.6. Are you thirsty? Are you poor? Have you inclined your ear and heard? Have you beheld the great Messiah, Christ Jesus? Then **'Seek ye the Lord while he may be found, call ye upon him while he is near.'** Bartimaeus did; the woman with the issue of blood did; the thief did! What is it to seek the Lord?

1. It is to discover that by nature I do not have him and I need his grace.

2. It is to desire his mercy and fellowship with him more than all.

3. It is to be made willing to be saved on his terms, that he might be just and justifier.

4. It is to be willing to part with all that is opposed to Christ.

5. It is to seek him, not his. If we have him, we have that which is his.

vv.7-9. Our thoughts are not God's thoughts, and our ways are not God's ways. This is evident in all things. But the main reference here is concerning God's thoughts and God's way of redeeming sinners! Our thoughts and ways, which seem right to the natural mind, are the ways of works and will lead to death. Naaman, when confronted with God's way, said, 'I thought...' Do you think that God can accept our imperfect righteousness, or pardon a sinner without justice being fully honoured? Suppose he did. Suppose that without Christ's righteousness and blood God accepted you. What peace could you have?

1. A god who could pardon without justice may one day condemn without reason.

2. A god who could set aside his righteousness may one day set aside his mercy.

3. A god who could deny his law may one day deny his gospel.

4. A god who could change his character may one day go back on his promises.

But the God of glory is never unjust in order to be gracious. He saves and accepts sinners, but not until Christ has honoured his law and satisfied his justice. This is God's way, and it is the way of peace and assurance!

vv. 10-11. As the rain and snow fall from heaven in their season and make the corn, wheat and vegetables to grow, and is not drawn up again into heaven but abides for a time on the earth to do the work for which it is sent, **'So shall my word be that goeth forth out of my mouth.'** His word of truth, his gospel of Christ, our Lord, and the sure mercies of David, which are contained therein, are sent forth into this world and shall not return until that word has accomplished that which he pleased and that for which he sent it — the salvation of his sheep (Isa. 46:9-11).

vv. 12-13. God's people shall go out of bondage with joy and be led forth in peace, without fear of ever being retaken by their enemy. Even the creation will rejoice with them and for them. Their land, once subject to the same bondage of sin, will be freed and partake in their redemption (Rom. 8:19-23). In all this his name shall be exalted and glorified.

36. The person and work of the Messiah

Isaiah 61:1-3

Isaiah 61 should be read along with Luke 4:16-21. Word had come back to Nazareth concerning one whom they knew quite well — one who had been brought up in their town, working as a carpenter. They had heard of some of the great things he had done and said (Luke 4:14-15,23). Now he was back in town, so they all gathered at the synagogue on the sabbath day, knowing that he would be there and would read and speak (Luke 4:16). Our Lord selected the Messianic prophecy from Isaiah 61:1-3, read it and declared, 'This day is this scripture fulfilled in your ears.'

If we can discover what this scripture is saying, we shall have an understanding of the person and work of our great Messiah. The people of Nazareth did not understand him or his ministry and sought to kill him (Luke 4:28-30). I pray that we understand the person and work of the Messiah.

v.1. **'The Spirit of the Lord God is upon me.'** Even the Saviour's mission and ministry were dependent on the Spirit of God (Mark 1:9-11; John 3:34-35). The Father ordained and anointed the God-man, Christ Jesus, to be our surety, substitute, sin-offering and Saviour. He gave him the Holy Spirit without measure. He came from the Father on behalf of his elect to accomplish the Father's will, speak his words, perform his work, honour his law and satisfy his justice.

'The Lord hath anointed me to preach good tidings unto the meek,' or the gospel to the poor. Our Lord preached (Matt. 4:17) by his words, his miracles, his silence and his looks. He lived the Prince of preachers, he died the theme of all preaching and he arose the Lord of preachers. He preached good tidings of grace, mercy and forgiveness of sin to the poor, not necessarily to the materially poor (for even the rich are poor spiritually), but to the poor in spirit. These are those who are sensible of their sins and humbled because of them. These poor disown any righteousness of their own and stand naked and condemned before God. These poor have nothing, know nothing and can do nothing acceptable unto God. They are in desperate need of all things and ascribe all that they receive to the grace of God.

'**He hath sent me to bind up the broken-hearted.**' A broken heart is painful and finds no relief for its distress in the flesh. A broken heart is helpless. We know what to do for a broken arm, but a broken heart needs a transplant — a new heart which only our Lord can give (Ps. 34:18; 51:17; Ezek. 36:25-27).

'**To proclaim liberty to the captives.**' In September 1862, Mr Lincoln issued an Emancipation Proclamation, effective from 1 January 1863, freeing all slaves. It was not a request, nor an invitation, nor a suggestion, but a proclamation — they were free! Our Lord came to set the captives of the law free from its curse, the captives of Satan and sin free from his dominion and from the penalty of sin (Rom. 8:33-34). By his grace, through his offering, we are free for ever (Heb. 10:12-14).

'**The opening of the prison to them that are bound.**' Believers, who have been bound by sin and in bondage to the flesh, are set free, but some are set free from the darkness and bondage of false religion, like Saul of Tarsus. False religion, tradition and legalism are a prison. We are delivered by Christ (Gal. 5:1).

v.2. '**To proclaim the acceptable year of the Lord.**' This is the fulfilment of the 'year of jubilee' (Lev. 25:8-10). Every seventh year was the Lord's year and was a sabbath of rest to the land. But the year following the seventh of these sevens was the year of jubilee. Every man sold into slavery was set free, all property and family land was redeemed and returned, all debts were discharged and a year of rest was proclaimed. Christ, our Kinsman-Redeemer, has done all of this for us. Our souls are free, our inheritance is restored, our debts are paid and we have entered into his rest for ever.

'**And the day of vengeance of our God.**' I know that many read this to be that awful day of vengeance when God was pleased to visit all the iniquity and transgressions of his people on Christ. It pleased the Lord to bruise him; he was smitten of God and afflicted. This is true, but the gospel is proclaimed with a twofold effect! All men do not believe. Some believed and some did not believe. The gospel preached is a fragrance of life to those who have life, but it is an odour of death and judgement to those who will not believe. God will visit his wrath upon those who will not believe (John 3:36; Mark 16:15-16; 2 Cor. 2:14-16). This is the day of vengeance of our God.

'**To comfort all that mourn.**' Christ is the true comfort for all true mourners. They mourn under a sense of sin (their own sins and the sins of others); they mourn under trial and affliction; they mourn when they cannot repent as they should, believe as they should, or pray as they should. But they find comfort for all this in Christ, his blood, his intercession and the precious promises of his Word.

v.3. '**To give ... them beauty for ashes.**' Ashes mean *the fire has gone out.* Our fire of joy, life and hope is burned out in Adam, but Christ restores the beauty and warmth of spiritual fire. Ashes mean *death*: 'Dust to dust and ashes to ashes.' In Christ we have eternal life, never to die. Ashes represent *sorrow.* In extreme sorrow there were ashes and sackcloth. But he took our death, our mourning, and bore our sorrows, giving to us beauty — his beauty (Ezek. 16:14).

'**Beauty for ashes, the oil of joy for mourning, the garment of praise for the spirit of heaviness.**' Here is what Isaiah is saying: the Lord Jesus gives his mourners the beautiful garments of his salvation, the robe of his righteousness, the graces of his Spirit and his gracious presence, together with his Word; and these yield joy, peace and comfort through all of this pilgrim journey.

'**That they might be called trees of righteousness, the planting of the Lord, that he might be glorified.**' Several things are suggested:

1. Trees are planted by someone. These are 'the planting of the Lord' (Matt. 15:13).
2. Trees that live have roots in water (Matt. 13:6; Ps. 1:3). Our root is in Christ, the living water.
3. The life of the tree is the sap within. The Spirit of God dwells in believers (John 7:37-39).
4. Trees which God plants bear fruit (Gal. 5:22).
5. Trees which God plants never wither (Ps. 1:3-4).

And in all of this God is glorified! From Alpha to Omega in the redemption of a sinner, God is glorified (John 17:1-4).

37. The Lord our righteousness

Jeremiah 23:1-8

This scripture is so applicable to our day that it could have been written this morning. The prophet deals with four powerful and present truths!

1. He pronounces woe and judgement on false preachers and pastors (vv.1-2).
2. He promises that God's elect will be called out of all nations and true shepherds and pastors will feed them (vv.3-4).
3. He presents the Messiah, our Redeemer, the Lord Jesus, who is the hope of all believers and the message of every true preacher (vv.5-6).
4. He declares that in comparison with the salvation of Christ, the deliverance out of Egypt would not even be spoken of (vv.7-8).

vv.1-2. In all ages there have been false prophets and preachers. Our Lord called them 'wolves in sheep's clothing' (Matt. 7:15-16). Peter said there were false preachers in Israel and there shall be false preachers in the church, who bring in 'damnable heresies', and 'many shall follow' them (2 Peter 2:1-3). Paul called them 'ministers of Satan' (2 Cor. 11:13-15) and their message 'doctrines of devils' (1 Tim. 4:1-3). But no one spoke out more strongly against these false preachers than Jeremiah, the weeping prophet (Jer. 9:1).

1. He charged them all with greed and covetousness (Jer. 6:13; cf. Ezek. 34:1-3).
2. He said they give people a false peace (Jer. 6:14).
3. He charged them with denying God's judgement against sin (Jer. 14:13-14).

4. Their message is not the Word of God but rather their own thoughts (Jer. 23:16-17).

5. They preach their dreams and visions and keep God's Word from the people (Jer. 23:25-32).

The sad thing about this is that, because of the depravity and deceitfulness of the human heart, people prefer to hear the words of the false preachers rather than the Word of God (Jer. 5:31; John 3:19; 5:43; 2 Tim. 4:3).

vv.3-4. When we look about us at the vast religious organizations steeped in tradition, idolatry and false doctrine, when we behold the multitudes of people who claim to be Christians but who have no knowledge of the living God, no love for the Lord Jesus, no evidence of the new birth and no commitment to holiness, when we hear all of the popular preachers with their messages of works and free will, we are made to wonder with Elijah, 'Am I the only one left?' or to ask with the apostles, 'Lord, are there few that be saved?' But God says:

'I will gather ... my flock.' Our Lord has an elect people; never doubt it! The Father gave them to him (John 6:37-39; 17:2,9); they were chosen and given to him in eternity past (Eph. 1:3-6; 2 Thess. 2:13); Christ loved them and gave himself for them (John 10:14-16); they shall all be justified, called and glorified (Rom. 8:28-31).

'I will set up shepherds over them which shall feed them.' Election is not salvation; it is *unto* salvation. Those whom the Father has chosen, those whom the Son has redeemed must be quickened by the Holy Spirit (Eph. 2:1) through the Word (James 1:18; 1 Peter 1:23) preached by faithful preachers (Rom. 10:13-17). All must hear the gospel, repent, and believe that gospel (2 Thess. 2:13; Eph. 1:13-14; 1 Cor. 1:21; John 5:24; Rom. 1:16-17).

'They shall fear no more, nor be dismayed, neither shall they be lacking.' The true pastors will comfort them with God's promises in Christ and establish them in the Word of God, and they will grow in grace and the knowledge of Christ through the Word (Eph. 4:11-15).

vv.5-6. Here is the gospel, the good news, the children's bread, the hope of the believer and the central fact of all Scripture! Here is the summary of redemption and the one way God can be a just God and a Saviour (Rom. 3:25-26).

'**Behold, the days come.**' All days, events, promises and patterns before Jesus Christ came to earth pointed to that day in the fulness of time when he was born, and all days in the future look back to that hour in which he died for sinners.

'**The Lord ... will raise unto David a righteous branch.**' Salvation is of the Lord. The Father purposed, planned and sent the Son. It is the will of God that prepared him a body, made him the seed of David, the Son of man and our substitute (Heb. 10:7-10; Phil. 2:5-11).

The Lord raised up the king who executed '**judgement and justice in the earth**'. Jesus Christ is Son of Man and Son of God. Jesus Christ is the servant, bone of our bone and flesh of our flesh, and also God Almighty — King (Rom. 1:3-4; Isa. 9:6; 2 Cor. 5:19-21).

'**In his days Judah shall be saved, and Israel shall dwell safely.**' True Judah and Israel are not that Old Testament nation which was merely a national people and a picture. True Israel, the true seed of Abraham, are the elect of God in Christ out of every nation on earth (Rom. 2:28-29; Gal. 3:7,16,26-29). These will all be saved.

The name whereby our Lord is called is '**the Lord our righteousness**'. He is our righteousness, having by his perfect life imputed unto us the very holiness of God (Rom. 10:1-4). He is our justification, having honoured and satisfied every demand of justice by his death. It is his name that saves, his name upon which we call and his name by which we are called the righteousness of God! (Jer. 33:16).

vv.7-8. '**Behold, the days come,**' and are here in Christ, when the people of God, redeemed by Christ and rejoicing in his grace, will no more talk of the deliverance out of Egypt by the hand of Moses, but will speak only of the Lord Jesus our righteousness, who has delivered us from the wrath to come by his perfect life and precious blood. What is the deliverance from Egypt, when compared to the effectual deliverance of Christ from the curse of the law?

All hail the power of Jesus' name,
Let angels prostrate fall;
Bring forth the royal diadem
And crown him Lord of all.

38. The believer's hope

Lamentations 3:1-26

Someone said, 'God has hedged us about on the one side with his promises of mercy, lest we despair, and he has hedged us about on the other side with warnings, lest we presume.' John Newton could sing,

> Amazing grace, how sweet the sound
> That saved a wretch liked me!

and he also wrote,

> 'Tis a point I long to know,
> Oft it gives me anxious thought;
> Do I love the Lord or no,
> Am I his, or am I not?

The apostle Paul urged all believers to 'Examine yourselves, whether ye be in the faith' (2 Cor. 13:5). Peter wrote, 'Give diligence to make your calling and election sure' (2 Peter 1:10).

What and who is the believer's hope? When we think upon our beginning in Adam's transgressions, of our nature of sin and our inability to think or do anything pleasing to God, how can we entertain a blessed hope of eternal life and glory? Jeremiah sets forth our hope as it always has been, is now and ever shall be. Our hope is in our Redeemer!

vv.1-18. As one reads these lamentations of Jeremiah before the holy God of heaven, one comes to the same conclusion as Jeremiah in verse 18: **'My strength and my hope is perished from the Lord,'** or as Isaiah said when he saw the Lord in his holiness and himself in his uncleanness, 'I am cut off; there is no strength or hope in me.'

vv.19-20. 'When I remember, or call to mind, my afflictions, my misery and the corruption of my nature and flesh, my soul is humbled and bowed down within me.' There is no way that a man who has seen God in his holiness, and the law of God in its perfect requirements, can look within himself or at his works and find any comfort or hope. A true sight of self in the presence of God can only convict us, humble us and crush us.

v.21. **'This I recall to ... mind.'** What — my works? No, his grace! What — my sins and misery? No, his love and mercy! Jeremiah has looked within and can only grieve, but now he looks to Christ and he shouts, **'Therefore have I hope!'**

vv.22-26. This blessed hope is sixfold.

1. **It is of the Lord's mercies that we are not consumed.'** In David's psalm of repentance (Ps. 51), he does not ask for justice but for mercy: 'Have mercy upon me, O God.' He said that God would be just to condemn him (Ps. 51:4). In Psalm 130 the same theme is repeated: if God should mark iniquity, none should stand, but with the Lord there is forgiveness and mercy (Ps. 130:3-4). Mercy is totally undeserved (Eph. 2:1-4); mercy is sovereign (Rom. 9:15-16); mercy is in Christ (Titus 3:5-7). We deserve condemnation; our hope is that God will be merciful to us in Christ.

2. **'His compassions fail not. They are new every morning.'** God is love, and his love for his people will never fail. His love is of old and everlasting, yet it is so fresh that it is new every morning. We are such unloving and unlovely creatures that it is difficult for us to comprehend the love of God in Christ for his elect.

> Love begins with God. We did not love God but rather hated him, yet he loved us (1 John 4:10,19).
> His love is unchanging (Mal. 3:6; Rom. 8:38-39).
> His love is infinite (John 3:16; 15:12-13).

Nothing I have done caused God to love me, and nothing that I have done, or will do, will make God cease to love me. This is our hope!

3. **'Great is thy faithfulness.'** We hear much preaching that exhorts us to be faithful stewards of the grace of God, faithful givers, faithful in worship, prayer and holiness, but our hope of life and glory is not in *our* faithfulness but in *his* faithfulness! We will be faithful by his grace and because he has given us a new heart which desires to walk with him, but even when we fail, fall and falter, he is faithful.

> God is faithful to himself and his Word (Num. 23:19; Isa. 46:9-11).
> God is faithful to his covenant (Rom. 8:29-31; Jer. 32:38-40).
> God is faithful to his Son (John 6:37-39; 17:1-3,24).

This was David's comfort when he lay dying — not in his faith, his works, or his service, but in God's faithfulness to his covenant (2 Sam. 23:5).

4. **'The Lord is my portion ... therefore will I hope in him.'** Aaron is a picture of the believer in this matter . 'The Lord spake unto Aaron, Thou shalt have no inheritance in their land, neither shalt thou have any part among them: I am thy part and thine inheritance' (Num. 18:20). As our Father, Husband, Brother and Friend, he has undertaken our total care spiritually, physically and materially. He is our portion, part and inheritance (1 Cor. 1:30; Matt. 6:31-34). If the Lord indeed, by his own choice and by God-given faith, is my portion, therefore will I hope in him.

5. **'The Lord is good unto them that wait for him, to the soul that seeketh him.'** Do you suppose there could ever be found one who sincerely waited upon God, sought his mercy in Christ and called upon him for mercy who did not receive his grace? God forbid! 'I sought the Lord, and then I knew that it was he that sought me; I waited and found the Lord, and afterward I knew that it was he who found me.' He is eternally good and gracious to all who call upon him, for in Christ he purposed to be. This is our hope — the Lord is good!

6. We **'hope and quietly wait for the salvation of the Lord'**. These last five words are also the hope Jonah expressed from the belly of the fish: 'Salvation is the Lord' (Jonah 2:9). We rejoice in his mercy, his love, his faithfulness, his sufficiency and his goodness, but in these five words the whole of the matter is summed up: 'Salvation is of the Lord.' This is the believer's hope. It is of the Lord in its planning, its execution, its application, its sustaining power and in its ultimate perfection (Ps. 65:4).

39. From nothing to everything

Ezekiel 16:1-4

The great, powerful and glorious nation of Israel (that arose to such splendour and beauty in the days of David and Solomon) started with one lone man — Abraham. And when God called him, he was an idolater in a heathen land (Josh. 24:2-3). Think of it — Abraham, well on in years, with no children and his wife past the age of child-bearing. From him came this mighty nation — from nothing to everything by the grace of God (Deut. 7:6-8) and by the power of God (Jer. 18:1-6). According to verses 10-14, their beauty was perfect through his beauty, which he put upon them.

But our chief business is not with national Israel but to see what this scripture shows us about ourselves, spiritual Israel, and the kingdom of our Lord. All that the Lord God did in Israel is a picture and type of his grace to us (spiritual Israel) in Christ, for 'They which are of faith, the same are the children of Abraham' (Gal. 3:7). 'He is a Jew, which is one inwardly' (Rom. 2:28-29).

1. What we were

vv.3-5. I am told that among some of the pagan nations, there was a terrible custom of leaving unwanted, deformed infants in the fields to perish. You will find no better picture of our state at birth in Adam than the story of this infant.

We were born in sin of fallen parents (Ps. 51:5; 58:3). We did not come into the world as those who might stand or fall, but as those who had already fallen.

Ours was a state of total depravity and total inability (Rom. 5:12). This newborn child is helpless, hopeless and without any power or ability to help itself. All it can do is cry until it perishes (Eph. 2:12).

No outside help is available (v.5). **'None eye pitied thee.'** The law must condemn, holiness is offended, truth is sworn to testify against us and justice bares its sword to destroy.

This is a loathsome sight but a true picture of fallen sinners! As Isaiah said, 'From the sole of the foot even unto the head there is no soundness in it, but wounds, and bruises and putrefying sores' (Isa. 1:6). If there is any help for such awful creatures as we are, it must come from our God (Rom. 3:10-26).

2 . What God did

vv.3-5. **'I passed by thee.'** We did not seek him; he sought us! We did not choose him; he chose us! We did not come where he is; he came to us where we were! He was mindful of us and set his love upon us before the world began and he entered into a covenant of mercy on our behalf with Jesus Christ, our surety (2 Thess. 2:13; Eph. 1:3-4; Heb. 13:20-21). He came where we were in the person of his Son (2 Cor. 5:19; Matt. 1:21-23), took our nature, obeyed the law (Gal. 4:4-5), took our sins and shame upon himself and redeemed us to God by his blood (1 Peter 3:18).

'I ... saw thee polluted in thine own blood.' He saw us as we really are, yet he loved us! Mercy is for the miserable, grace is for the guilty and salvation is for real sinners (Matt. 9:10-13). 'But God commended his love toward us, in that, while we were yet sinners, Christ died for us' (Rom. 5:6,8,10).

'I said unto thee, when thou wast in thy blood, Live.' In the same way that our Lord stood before the grave of Lazarus (who stank) and called him forth to life, he quickens us (dead sinners) and makes us to live in him (Eph. 2:1; John 5:21). When our Lord brings a sinner to life through his Word (James 1:18), death gives way to life, darkness becomes light, inability gives way to strength and our enemies flee away. The same power that raised Christ from the grave raised us (Eph. 1:9-20).

3. What we are now

vv.8-14. **'It was the time of love,'** not our love for, but his love for us (1 John 4:10). 'We love him, because he first loved us' (1 John 4:19).

'I ... covered thy nakedness.' He took away our reproach, our shame and our guilt and made us righteous and holy in Christ (Jer. 23:5-6; 2 Cor. 5:21).

'Then washed I thee with water.' He cleansed us with water and blood.

> Let the water and the blood,
> From thy riven side which flowed,
> Be of sin the double cure [justify and sanctify],
> Save from wrath and make me pure.

'I clothed thee ... I decked [adorned] thee, ...I put ... a beautiful crown upon thine head.' 'Thou becamest mine!' By his grace, through the merits of our Lord Jesus, he has brought us from death to eternal life, from the pit of corruption and sin to perfect righteousness in him (Jude 24-25). Salvation is of the Lord, from the beginning to eternal glory.

Verse 14 declares, **'Thy beauty ... is perfect through my comeliness, which I had put upon thee.'** C. H. Spurgeon once said, 'The whole of the work whereby a lost sinner is lifted from the dunghill of sin, washed in the blood and made righteous, exalted to eternal life and glory is of the Lord and of him only.'

40. Lost, driven away, broken, sick

Ezekiel 34:1-6,11-17

The Lord has been pleased to use prophets, apostles, evangelists and pastor-teachers to preach the gospel of his grace to his people, that they may hear, believe and be converted (Eph. 4:10-14). 'It pleased God by the foolishness of preaching to save them that believe' (1 Cor. 1:21). While these men are called 'shepherds', the Lord Jesus is the Chief Shepherd, the Good Shepherd and our Great Shepherd. These under-shepherds labour as his servants, stewards of the grace of God, and as those who must give an account of their stewardship (Heb. 13:17; Luke 16:2).

Our text begins with the Lord's rebuking some unfaithful preachers who have not done what they were called to do.

v.2. Their first concern was for themselves and not for the sheep. Should not a true shepherd's first concern be for the well-being of his flock?

v.3. These preachers eat well, live well and are clothed and cared for by the sheep, but, while they take from the flock, they do not feed them the Word! Isaiah said, 'They all look to their own gain' (Isa. 56:11).

v.4. In this verse we encounter for the first time four words which are found later in this chapter to describe the ministry of our Chief Shepherd, the Lord Jesus! Here is the charge against the shepherds:'You have not **"sought that which was lost"**. You have not **"brought again that which was driven away"**. You have not **"bound up that which was broken"**. You have not **"healed that which was sick"**.'

If this is the ministry of the Chief Shepherd, then it should be our ministry. If this is the work of our Saviour God, then let us who preach and teach his Word, who are called to feed his sheep, study his person and work and be about our Master's business (John 10:14-16).

vv.11-16. He says, '**I will both search my sheep, and seek them out**' (v.11); '**I will feed them in a good pasture**' (v.14); '**I will feed my flock, and cause them to lie down**' (v.15). And, as he has always used faithful men, he will raise them up and send them to his sheep today! But the under-shepherds must understand the character of his sheep and the character of his gospel, which is given in verse 16 using these four words: 'lost, driven away, broken, sick'.

1. **'I will seek that which was lost.'** This is a term our Lord used often to refer to those whom he came to save. 'The Son of man is come to seek and to save that which was lost' (Luke 19:10; Matt. 10:6; 15:24). A lost sheep is away from the fold, separated from the shepherd's care, does not know the way back and has no power or ability to return to the fold. Paul describes us as 'without Christ ... having no hope, and without God' (Eph. 2:12).

The good news of the gospel is that our Lord will seek that which was lost. He came not to call the righteous but sinners to repentance (Matt. 9:10-13). He will seek and save the lost sheep and welcome home the lost son.

2. **'I will ... bring again that which was driven away.'** What took the sheep away from the shepherd? We are out in the wilderness of shame and iniquity, away from God. How did we get in this condition? 'Your iniquities have separated between you and your God, and your sins have hid his face from you' (Isa. 59:2). Firstly, the fall of Adam has driven us away from God (Rom. 5:12), and, secondly, our vain, religious ceremonies and attempts at self-righteousness have driven us away from God (Isa. 1:11-15; Rom. 10:1-3). Thank God, he will not leave us away from him, but our Lord Jesus died, 'the just for the unjust', to bring us to God (1 Peter 3:18).

3. **'I ... will bind up that which was broken.'** Read Psalm 34:18 and Psalm 51:17. Is that which is broken good for anything? One cannot see in a broken mirror; one cannot drink from a broken glass; one cannot use a broken arm; one cannot walk with a broken cane.

Only the heart is at its best state when it is broken:

It is acceptable and well-pleasing to God (Ps. 51:17).
It makes up for defects in our duties (Ps. 51:17).
The Lord is nigh unto the broken heart (Ps. 34:18).
The Lord will save the broken heart (Ps. 34:18).
God dwells with the broken heart (Isa. 57:15).

A broken heart implies a godly sorrow over sin, is humble before God, claiming no merit or goodness, and yields sweet fragrance like a sweet shrub when it is crushed.

4. **'I ... will strengthen that which was sick.'** It is true that the Lord sometimes heals his people when they are ill, and sometimes he does not. He is able to deliver us from any distress, trial or trouble if it is his will to do so. But our sickness in this scripture is a spiritual sickness called sin, iniquity and transgression. Isaiah's prophecy in Isaiah 53:4 declares, 'Himself took our infirmities, and bare our sicknesses' (Matt. 8:17). Also, 'By his stripes we are healed' (Isa. 53:5). This is not teaching that our bodies will not be sick because of his atonement. We shall endure physical suffering, pain and death, but not our souls. They are perfectly healed and whole from all disease, sin and death. He that believes on the Son shall never die (John 11:25-26) because 'By his stripes we are healed,' perfectly whole for ever.

v. 17. One word must be added. While our Lord delights to show mercy to the lost, driven away, broken-hearted and sick, he will destroy those who think that they are fat, strong and have no need. Luke 9:11 says, 'He ... healed them that had need of healing.'

41. 'Can these bones live?'

Ezekiel 37:1-14

There are at least three things taught in these verses.

1. This scripture is a prophecy of the restoration of Israel as a nation, and some say the conversion of many of them. Charles Spurgeon wrote in 1864, 'There will be a native government again. The state of Israel will be incorporated. The Jews shall return to Palestine and walk upon her mountains and sit under her fig trees.'

2. This scripture is a description of the resurrection of the dead. I have watched as the bones of the dead in Mexico have been transferred from a grave to the family box, and in amazement I have wondered, 'Can these bones live?' Our Lord said that they will all live again (John 5:28-29).

3. But as all of the Old Testament Scriptures 'testify of Christ' (John 5:39; Luke 24:27), this scripture is a picture of the resurrection of dead sinners to eternal life through, and by the grace and power of, our Lord Jesus Christ (Eph. 2:1; Col. 2:13; 1 Cor. 15:22). The giving of life and salvation to dead sinners is a greater miracle than the restoration of Israel or the resurrection of dead bodies. The two greatest mysteries and miracles are, first, that the Son of God became the Son of Man and, second, that the sons of men, by his grace, become the sons of God! (1 Tim. 3:16; 1 John 3:1).

1. Here is the truth about human nature — it is dead in sin

vv.1-2. Do you want to know the truth about our fallen state? Do you want to see what we really are as a result of Adam's transgression? (Rom. 5:12). Here it is! Evidently there had been a battle fought in this valley years before, and many men were killed. Their bones lay scattered about in the sand, bleached white, so dry and parched a dog would not pick one up. All the moisture and marrow had been gone out of them for years. They were very many and very dry.

Martin Luther once said, 'If a man could get a full view of his sin and lost condition as it really is, he would lose his sanity.' Like these dry bones, by nature we are without help, without hope, without Christ and without God in this world (Eph. 2:12). The dead sinner cannot feel, will, fear, love, repent, or believe because he is devoid of spiritual life. He is dead!

2. 'Can these bones live?'

v.3. This is the question the Lord God put to the prophet. Can men with blood, breath and bodies stand where these bones lie in the dust?

This is the whole issue of Scripture. Can the Ethiopian change his skin, or the leopard his spots? Can we do good that are accustomed to do evil? (Jer. 13:23). Can the fragrance of the rose issue forth from the sepulchre? Can the cursing tongue praise the Lord? Can hate be turned to love, and pride and arrogance to humility?

The prophet gave the only answer: **'O Lord God, thou knowest.'** The preacher certainly has no power to accomplish such a miracle. The bones have no power to raise themselves. So a dead sinner has no more power to give himself spiritual life than a dead body can raise itself. Our Lord said, 'No man can come to me, except the Father which hath sent me draw him' (John 6:44). No man will move towards God until God moves him. By nature we not only have no power to live, but we have no desire nor will to live. 'Thy people [are made] willing in the day of thy power' (Ps. 110:3).

3. The command comes from the Lord to preach to the bones

v.4. **'Prophesy upon these bones, and say unto them, O ye dry bones, hear the word of the Lord.'** I suppose if someone wanted dry, dead bones to live, the very last thing he would consider doing would be to preach to them. But this is God's way and God's command: 'Preach the word of the Lord to them' (1 Cor. 1:21; Rom. 1:16; 10:13-17; James 1:18).

The Word of God is the word of life.

Christ is the Word of God, and one cannot separate the Word incarnate from the Word written and spoken.

Life-giving sermons are sermons filled with Christ — his person, his obedience, his blood, his resurrection, his exaltation and his intercession (Acts 13:38-39; 2 Cor. 5:18-21).

When Christ is preached (who he is, what he did, why he did it and where he is), those who are given ears to hear do indeed hear Christ (John 13:20). The Holy Spirit and the Word of God bring life (1 Peter 1:23). This is why the apostle Paul determined to know nothing among them except Jesus Christ and him crucified (1 Cor. 2:2), for this gospel preached is the power of God to salvation (Rom. 1:16).

4. The message that God gave Ezekiel to preach rang of free and sovereign grace

vv.5-6 The message was not an appeal to the bones to do something for God, but it was a proclamation of what God was pleased to do for them. **'I will cause breath to enter into you, and ye shall live... I will lay sinews upon you, and will bring up flesh upon you, and cover you with skin ... and ye shall know that I am the Lord'** (cf. Isa. 45:22).

The word is not 'I will if you will,' but rather God says, 'I will ... and you shall!' God's will and purpose are not subject to man's depraved will. He works all things after the counsel of his will and makes us willing (Eph. 1:11).

Through the years preachers have been exhorted not to preach God's sovereignty, covenant mercies, elective grace and effectual, particular redemption to sinners; but these are the very truths God instructed the prophet to preach to these dead bones. Tell them who God is, what they are and what God is pleased to do for them in Christ Jesus (Eph. 1:3-14).

5. The results of preaching the gospel of God's glory

vv.7-10. **'So I prophesied as I was commanded.'** Wouldn't it be refreshing if all preachers would forget the programmes, the entertainment, the methods, the eloquence and preach the Word of God as they are commanded!

'**There was a noise,**' or a stir! If the true Word of God is preached in the power of God's Spirit, there will be a stir — the stir of interest, of life, of joy, of faith. But there will also be the stir of opposition, persecution and trouble.

'**Come..., O breath, and breathe upon these slain, that they may live.**' Ezekiel did more than just preach: he prayed to the Spirit of the Lord to give life (John 3:5-8). Doctrines and facts (as true as they are) do not save or give life. Christ is our life, and he must give life! He said, 'I am the resurrection and the life; he that believeth in me, though he were dead, yet shall he live' (John 11:25).

42. Four things God taught Nebuchadnezzar

Daniel 4:28-37

Those who know the living God, who have seen a little of his glory and majesty in the face of Christ Jesus, are troubled by the low opionion that men today have of God. 'There is no fear of God before their eyes' (Rom. 3:18). 'Thou thoughtest that I was altogether such an one as thyself' (Ps. 50:21). Such trash and triviality are permitted in the pulpit and church in the name of God, and such familiarity, irreverence, small thoughts and loose talk about the Lord God, as are unheard of in the Scriptures or among our ancient fathers. Let us look at the text and see how the Lord dealt with Nebuchadnezzar and what he was pleased to teach him.

No one ever accused Nebuchadnezzar of being a prophet, but the Lord taught him, as he taught Jonah, some powerful truth in a most unusual way. Nebuchadnezzar was a great and powerful man, and also a very proud man (Dan. 4:22-30). Becuase of his pride and boasting, the Lord took away his kingdom and his understanding and he became like an animal for a time (vv. 32-33). Through this experience he learned four things.

1. He learned the majesty, greatness and sovereignty of God

v. 34. At the end of those days, Nebuchadnezzar said, **'I praised and honoured him that liveth for ever, whose dominion is an everlasting dominion.'**

When Moses stood before the bush that burned and was not consumed and asked, 'What is thy name?' the Lord said to Moses, 'I AM THAT I AM.' There was a time when man was not; there was a time when the world was not; there was a time when the heavens were not; there was a time when time was not; but our God is, was and ever shall be. 'I praised him that liveth for ever.'

The Lord God's dominion and reign are everlasting, infinite, irresistible and immutable. The hymn-writer wrote:

Thy throne eternal ages stood,
Ere seas or stars were made;
Thou art the ever-living God,
Were all the nations dead.

Eternity, with all its years,
Stands present in thy view;
To thee there's nothing old appears—
Great God, there's nothing new!

Let idols topple to the ground
And their own worshippers confound,
But Judah shout and Zion sing
And each confess our sovereign King.

He is absolutely sovereign in *creation*. All things were made by him and for him, and by him they are held together. By him they shall be destroyed, and he will make 'all things new' (Rev. 21:5; 2 Peter 3:10-13).

He is totally sovereign in *providence*. Not a bird falls to the ground without him. He 'worketh all things after the counsel of his own will' (Matt. 10:29; Eph. 1:11; Isa. 45:5-7; 46:9-11). He so orders all events, all men and their actions that 'All things work together for good to them that love him and are the called according to his purpose.'

He is sovereign in *salvation*. He said to Moses, 'I will have mercy on whom I will have mercy' (Rom. 9:10-18; 8:28-31). Our Lord said, 'The Son quickeneth whom he will' (John 5:21).

How did David identify the Lord God when the heathen asked, 'Where is your God?' He replied, 'Our God is in the heavens: he hath done whatsoever he hath pleased' (Ps. 115:2-3).

2. He learned that man is nothing

v. 35. **'And all the inhabitants of the earth are reputed as nothing.'** '*All* the inhabitants of the earth are ... as nothing' — not some, not the poor, the rich, the weak, the openly wicked, but all together. Kings, emperors, the rich, the powerful, the learned, the talented, the wise and the foolish are all before him as nothing. Men came from the earth and will return to the earth. 'We brought nothing into this world, and ... we can carry nothing out' (1 Tim. 6:7). Without him we can do nothing! (John 15:5).

Isaiah wrote, 'All nations before him are as nothing; and they are counted to him less than nothing.' We are a 'drop of the bucket'. This is the unnoticed drop of liquid which falls from a bucket when it is emptied. We are 'counted as the small dust of the balance'. This is the dust upon the scales which does not affect the weight or the outcome (Isa. 40:15-17)

This knowledge of who God is and what we are enables us to praise God and give him all the glory for the mercy and grace he gives us in Christ Jesus. This knowledge made David to exclaim, 'What is man, that thou art mindful of him?' (Ps. 8:3-4). It made Paul say, 'O wretched man that I am! Who shall deliver me from this body of death? I thank God through Jesus Christ our Lord' (Rom. 7:24-25).

3. He learned that the will of God is unchangeable and shall be done

v.35. 'He doeth according to his will in the army of heaven, and among the inhabitants of the earth: and none can stay his hand, or say unto him, What doest thou?' Only God has a free will! One may argue about 'my will, your will, free will, and whosoever will'; but in this universe there is one sovereign, immutable will, and that is the will of God. 'Thy will be done in earth, as it is in heaven.' Even men such as Pharaoh (Rom. 9:17), Judas (John 17:12) and those who crucified Christ (Acts 4:27-28), doing what their perverted wills wanted to do, were at the same time fulfilling God's will (Acts 13:29).

David said, 'Whatsoever the Lord pleased, that did he in heaven, and in earth, in the seas, and all deep places' (Ps. 135:6). What has it pleased God to do?

> 'It ... pleased the Lord to make you his people' (1 Sam. 12:22).
> 'It pleased the Father that in [Christ] should all fulness dwell' (Col. 1:19).

'It pleased the Lord to bruise [Christ]' (Isa. 53:10).

'It pleased God ... to reveal his Son' in us (Gal. 1:15).

'It pleased God by the foolishness of preaching to save them that believe' (1 Cor. 1:21).

4. *He learned that those who walk in pride the Lord is able to abase*

v.37. Over and over in the Scripture the Lord has revealed his wrath against pride. Pride is the first on the list of seven things which God hates (Prov. 6:16-19). He will turn away the proud and bless the humble (James 4:6).

May it please God to have mercy upon us according to his lovingkindness and his tender mercies, to blot out our transgressions, to create in us a clean heart and a right spirit and to save us for Christ's sake!

43. 'Thy God will deliver thee'

Daniel 6:1-24

Daniel, the prophet of God who was in captivity, had interpreted the handwriting on the wall for King Belshazzar. Because of this, Daniel was clothed with scarlet, a gold chain was put on his neck and he was made the third ruler in the kingdom (Dan. 5:25-29). That night Belshazzar was slain and Darius became the king.

vv.1-3. Darius set over the kingdom 120 princes and over these princes he established three presidents, of whom Daniel was the chief president. The king respected and admired Daniel **'because an excellent spirit was in him'**, and he planned to set him over the whole realm.

vv.4-9. The other presidents and princes were jealous and envious of Daniel and desired to find a reason whereby Daniel could be discredited before the king. But they could find no fault with this faithful man. They finally decided that the only area in which Daniel could be charged would be concerning his love for the faith in the true and living God. Though Daniel was in a pagan society and surrounded by idolatrous people, he worshipped, prayed three times daily and gave thanks before God (v.10).

Pretending to honour King Darius, these wicked men drew up a decree (they called it a royal statute) that for thirty days if any person in the kingdom should pray or ask a petition from any god or man, except King Darius, he would be cast into the den of lions. They knew that in this way they could trap Daniel, for he would never go even a day without prayer. The king was fooled and flattered by these men and signed the degree **'that it be not changed, according to the law of the Medes and Persians, which altereth not'** (v.8).

vv.10-17. Daniel prayed and gave thanks to God, as he did every day. Then these men reported Daniel to the king and reminded the king of his decree. Darius was displeased with himself and, because he admired Daniel, **'he laboured till the going down of the sun to deliver him'** (v.14). There was nothing that Darius could do: the law was established; Daniel had violated the law and the sentence must be carried out. The king commanded Daniel to be cast into the den of lions and said unto him, **'Thy God, whom thou servest continually, he will deliver thee.'**

vv.18-24. The Lord did indeed deliver Daniel from the lions. Daniel told Darius, **'My God hath sent his angel, and hath shut the lions' mouths, that they have not hurt me.'** Then the king brought those men who had accused Daniel and put them in the den of lions.

This is an Old Testament picture of our deliverance from the judgement and curse of the law of God, which we have broken. Consider these things:

1. The law of God cannot be changed; it does not alter

Unlike Darius' law, which was a foolish one, God's law is holy and just and good (Rom. 7:12). It is a revelation of the holiness and righteousness of our God.

God's law is spiritual and requires not only outward obedience but inward perfection (Rom. 7:14; Matt. 5:21-28). There are no loopholes and no compromise. 'Cursed is everyone that continueth not in all things which are written in the book of the law to do them!' (Gal. 3:10).

2. We have broken God's law

The law of King Darius, which Daniel violated, was a wicked law and should have been disregarded by a true believer, but the laws of our God should be kept; but we have not, do not and cannot in this flesh obey them perfectly. Sin is the transgression of God's law and we are all transgressors, sinners and workers of iniquity (Rom. 3:10-19; Ps. 14:1-3). And, like Darius, we may labour all our lives (till the going down of life's sun) to establish a righteousness, to appease a holy God, or to escape the just condemnation of our sins, but it cannot be done! God will and must carry out sentence and judgement against our sins (Ezek. 18:20).

3. 'Thy God, he will deliver thee'

Darius could not find a way to deliver Daniel from his law. But our Father purposed a way to honour his law, to satisfy his justice (without compromising his holiness) and a way whereby he could be just and the justifier of sinners (Rom. 3:19-26). The Lord Jesus Christ, the God-man (1 Tim. 3:16), came into this world, 'made of a woman, made under the law,' to redeem them who had broken the law (Gal. 4:4). By his perfect obedience he imputed to us his righteousness. By his death (1 Peter 3:18; Isa. 53:4-6) he took our sins and 'paid it all, all the debt we owe. Sin has left a crimson stain, but he washed it white as snow.' Our God delivered us literally by going into 'the den of lions' for us. He did not come to destroy his law, but to fulfil it, not to find a way around justice, but to meet it (bearing our sins) and satisfy it in full!

> Who can be in the form of God and take the form of a servant?
> Who can come to the earth in flesh and never leave the bosom of the Father?
> Who can be holy, harmless, undefiled, separate from sinners, yet be numbered with them?
> Who can be tempted in all points of the law, yet be without sin?
> Who can die, be buried and walk out of the tomb victoriously under his own power?
> Who can ascend to heaven and be commanded to sit at the right hand of majesty and yet be a man?
> Who? The God-man, our Lord Jesus Christ!

This is the gospel of substitution and satisfaction. Christ, our substitute, made full satisfaction to the law and the justice of God on our behalf.

44. Hosea — a type of Christ

Hosea 1-3

The name 'Hosea' is the same as Joshua and Jesus and signifies a saviour or a deliverer. Hosea was not only a faithful prophet and servant of the Lord, but he is a powerful type and picture of our Lord Jesus in his love and mercy to sinners. It is surprising that we do not hear more sermons on Hosea, since he has such a name and his writings are so filled with grace for the guilty.

1. The story in brief

God commanded Hosea to take a wife from among the people of whoredom. Fornication and adultery were their way of life. Hosea married Gomer, who was quite young, and she bore him three children. Then Gomer began to walk the way of her heritage, leaving Hosea for her lovers. Even though she had left him and was living in wickedness and shame, Hosea continued to provide corn, wine, oil and money for her. Gomer thought these gifts were from her lovers, and she praised them. Soon she was brought down to poverty, shame and loneliness and was to be sold on the block as a common slave. Hosea loved her yet, and he went to the marketplace and bought her for the price demanded and took her home to be his wife, no more to leave.

2. The key to this story

'Then said the Lord unto me, Go yet, love a woman beloved of her friend ... according to the love of the Lord toward the children of Israel, who look to other gods, and love flagons of wine' (Hosea 3:1). The Lord put Hosea through this unusual experience to demonstrate his grace, love and mercy to his people, all of whom have sinned and gone astray, turning to our own way. We did not love him, but he loved us with an 'everlasting love' and 'loved us to the end'.

1:1-3. According to the commandment of the Lord, Hosea went among a vile race, a sinful people, and took his bride, joining himself to her as one!

Our Lord chose his bride from Adam's fallen, sinful race (1 Cor. 1:26-29; Rom. 5:6-8; Eph. 2:1-5).

We did not love him; he loved us (1 John 4:10). We did not choose him; he chose us (John 15:16). We did not deserve his mercy and love. The cause of his love for us and our redemption is found only in himself, not in us!

2:1-5. A short time after their marriage, Gomer left Hosea and followed the ways of her people. She was from a people of whoredom and when she became of full age, she walked the same path they walked.

Though our God entered a covenant with Christ, chose us in Christ and made us his own before the world began (Eph. 1:3-6; 2 Thess. 2:13; Gal. 1:15), we were born into this world sons of Adam, fallen sinners, and we go astray from the womb (Ps. 51:5; 58:3; Jer. 13:23; Rom. 5:12,19).

We do not come into the world as those who might fall; we are born already fallen and only have to reach a certain age and be exposed to certain temptations to reveal what we already are! We are not sinners because we sin; we sin because we are sinners (Rom. 3:10-19). It is our nature to love sin and hate holiness.

2:5-8. Hosea took care of Gomer even in her rebellion and sin. She said, **'I will go after my lovers that gave me my bread and my water, my wool and my flax... She did not know that I gave her'** these things.

Oh, how gracious the Lord is to his people all the days of our lives! From our birth and all the days of our lives he has protected us, provided for us and blessed us, even when we knew him not, nor desired to know him.

Like Gomer, we praise ourselves, talk about good luck, or give the glory to the flesh, and do not know that our Lord is the giver of every good gift (Rom. 8:28-31; Gal. 1:15).

2:9-11. Finally, Gomer was brought low; her life became a burden; her joy was turned to mourning; the sweetness became bitter; that which she had loved, she hated.

The Lord God will bring his people to this place. A sinner must be lost to be saved; he must be brought low before he can be lifted up and exalted; he must, like Gomer and the prodigal son, discover what he is, where he is, and feel the guilt, shame and burden of sin (John 6:44-45).

We cannot taste of grace until we weary of sin. We will not love and flee to Christ until we hate our fleshly lovers and what they have done to us. To miss conviction of sin is to miss repentance, and to miss repentance is to miss faith, and to miss faith is to miss Christ. The Holy Spirit of God, in bringing us to repentance towards God and faith in Christ Jesus, will convince us of sin, righteousness and judgement (John 16:8-11).

3:1-3. Gomer belonged to the fallen system! She was in the clutches and possession of her masters. There was a price on her head. Hosea bore the shame of identification with her and, revealing his special care for her, paid the price and set her free.

We belonged to a fallen humanity; we were in the possession of the law and justice. There was a price on our heads — eternal condemnation, curse and death (Isa. 53:4-6,10-12).

Christ loved us, was numbered with us and, 'despising the shame, he endured the cross,' and paid what we owed but could not pay. 'He paid a debt he did not owe for us who owed a debt we could not pay.'

Hosea 3:3 reveals the security of the Lord's purchased bride and her eternal union with him (John 10:24-30). This is the covenant revealed in Jeremiah: 'They shall be my people, and I will be their God... I will not turn away from them, to do them good ... they shall not depart from me' (Jer. 32:38-40; Mal. 3:6; Phil. 1-6).

45. A famine to be feared

Amos 8:11-13

The nation of Israel often disobeyed God, rebelling against his law and commandments. Yet the Lord continued to send his prophets to warn them, to instruct them and to call them. Though they were a stiff-necked people who erred in their hearts and did not know his ways (Ps. 95:10; Heb. 3:10), even followed other gods, yet the Lord owned them, restrained them and would not suffer them to be without 'a word from the Lord'.

Now in this chapter of Amos, the Lord announces judgement upon Israel, the very worst thing that can come upon them: 'I will take my word from you and there will be no message from the Lord' (Amos 8:11-13). If men are deprived of light, they wander in darkness. If men are deprived of truth, they walk in error. Judicial blindness and no word from God is our greatest fear. It was said of Ephraim, 'Leave him alone,' and of the Pharisees, 'Leave them alone' (Hosea 4:17; Matt. 15:14). Nothing could be worse.

David feared this and said, 'Take not thy Holy Spirit from me' (Ps. 51:11).

Jeremiah wrote, 'The prophets also find no vision from the Lord' (Lam. 2:9).

Micah said, 'There is no answer from God' (Micah 3:7).

Amos wrote, **'They shall run to and fro to seek the word of the Lord, and shall not find it'** (Amos 8:12).

These servants of God all feared for the people when the heavens were silent.

1. What are the signs of 'a famine of hearing the words of the Lord'?

Religion does not cease, for religion is as much a part of man as any emotion, as revealed in John 1:11: 'He came unto his own [nation,

priesthood and tabernacle], and his own received him not.' But
when there is a famine of hearing the word of the Lord:

> Ministers go on preaching but without the power of the
> Holy Spirit. The voice of a man is the only voice the people
> hear. The gospel is heard in 'word only' (1 Thess. 1:5); and
> there is no regeneration, no conviction, no revelation of
> Christ and no comfort or growth.

> Assemblies gather together on the Lord's Day, but the
> Lord is not present with them. Like Mary and Joseph, they
> travel a day's journey supposing Jesus to have been in the
> company (Luke 2:44), but he was not there and they sought
> him sorrowing.

> The Word of God is read, but there is no application to the
> heart. The disciples said, 'Did not our heart burn within us
> ... while he opened to us the scriptures?' (Luke 24:32). Dear
> friends, someone said, 'We have listened to the preacher;
> truth by him has been shown; but we need a great teacher
> from the everlasting throne: application is the work of God
> alone!'

> The ordinances (baptism and the Lord's Table) are ob-
> served, but they are meaningless rituals and ceremonies
> without him. The formality of prayer is kept up; but if the
> Lord God has no respect to the prayer of his servants, it is
> useless to pray (1 Kings 8:28).

> The famine and drought are at their height when the
> Scriptures become a source of controversy instead of com-
> fort, a source of debate instead of instruction and inspiration.
> When we are more concerned with proving our doctrine than
> proving ourselves, then our table becomes a snare and the
> means of salvation becomes a means of delusion (2 Thess.
> 2:10-12).

*2. By the grace of God, how can such a famine be prevented
in our area and in our day?*

I urge you to look at Psalm 51 — the seeking sinner's guide and the
believing sinner's comfort. God heard David when he lived and
prayed this psalm, and he will hear us when we do!

Ps. 51:1-2 — A plea for mercy. David pleads for mercy on the grounds of the Lord's lovingkindness and tender mercies. He does not claim any merit or righteousness, but he prays to be washed, cleansed and for his sins to be blotted out because 'There is forgiveness with thee,' and 'With him is plenteous redemption' (Ps. 130:4,7).

Ps. 51:3-4 — A confession of sin. You can be sure that there will be no forgiveness of sin, nor mercy from God, where there is no confession of sin. 'If we confess our sins, he is faithful and just to forgive' (1 John 1:9). 'He that covereth his sins shall not prosper: but whoso confesseth and forsaketh them shall have mercy' (Prov. 28:13). Note the openness and honesty of his confession: **'My sin is ever before me. Against thee ... have I sinned, and done ... evil in thy sight.'**

Verse 4 contains a solemn and important statement. David justifies God and takes sides with God against himself: 'You are just when you speak against my sin and you are clear when you judge and condemn me.' A truly repentant sinner will own that he deserves to be damned (Luke 7:29-30).

Ps. 51:5-6 — A reason for our troubles. Our great problem is not so much what we do as what we are. What we are (fallen, depraved, corrupt sinners) determines what we have done and what we do. David confesses that his problem is within. Not only is the water bad, the fountain is bad! We were conceived in sin and brought forth from the womb speaking lies (Ps. 58:3; Rom. 5:12). We need to be born again; we need a new heart and a new nature (John 3:3-8).

Ps. 51:7-8 — A remedy provided. The Roman church has a doctrine called purgatory, a place where all people go after death to be purged from their sins by suffering themselves or by the good works and prayers of loved ones on earth. In purgatory they are purged from sin and made ready for heaven. One thing is true in all of this: if we are to stand in God's presence, we must be purged from all sin. This is what David desires when he says, **'Purge me with hyssop, and I shall be clean.'** But David speaks of the blood atonement on the mercy-seat provided by the Lamb of God, our Lord Jesus Christ. The first mention in the Bible of hyssop was in Exodus 12:22 when the hyssop was dipped in the blood of the passover lamb and sprinkled on the door in Egypt. God said, 'When I see the blood, I will pass over you.' This is the message which brings blessings, the presence of God and good to his people. There will be no famine of the Word where there is:

1. A plea for God's mercy from the heart.
2. A genuine confession of sin.
3. An understanding of the root of our problem.
4. The preaching of Christ, our substitute, and him crucified.

Our God will honour those who honour his Son. Most of the time when there is a famine of the Word, the problem is not in the pew but in the pulpit. Where God's servants faithfully preach Christ Jesus, the Father will bless.

46. Salvation is of the Lord

Jonah 2:1-10

I do not know how much importance can be attached to this, or whether it is of any importance at all, but the word of the Lord first came to Jonah saying, 'Arise, go to Nineveh, that great city, *and cry against it*' (Jonah 1:2). Then, after he fled from the presence of the Lord, sailed to Tarshish, was swallowed by the fish and uttered these immortal words, **'Salvation is of the Lord,'** Jonah was told by the Lord, 'Arise, go unto Nineveh, that great city, and *preach unto it the preaching that I bid thee*' (Jonah 3:1-2). Crying against a city because of its wickedness does not require much knowledge, understanding, or compassion, but preaching the Lord's message of grace and salvation involves an understanding by experience and faith in that gospel and the glory of God. This Jonah received in the darkness and hopelessness of the fish's belly.

Moses declared unto the children of Israel, as they stood before the Red Sea with the thundering hosts of Egyptians descending upon them, 'Stand still, and see the salvation of the Lord' (Exod. 14:13; Ps. 3:8; 37:39; 62:1). Jahaziel told Israel, 'The battle is not yours, but God's... Stand ye still, and see the salvation of the Lord' (2 Chron. 20:15-17). Simeon prayed to die, for 'Mine eyes have seen thy salvation' (Luke 2:30). A man can only preach what he has experienced, and Jonah learned that 'Salvation is of the Lord.'

1. What do we mean by these words, 'Salvation is of the Lord'?

Someone wrote years ago, 'The royal bath of mercy, wherein black souls are washed white as the snow, was filled from the veins of our Lord Jesus Christ. No blood of martyrs mingled with that stream. No blood of noble confessors and heroes of the cross entered into that river of atonement. The atonement is the unaided work of the Lord of glory.' The banquet of mercy is served by one host, the Lord Jesus

Christ, who prepared the feast, invited the guests, made them willing to come and gave to them their robes of spotless righteousness. A preacher of the last century declared, 'My gospel is simply this: the whole of the work whereby a guilty, fallen son of Adam is lifted from the dunghill, washed, justified, and translated into the king-dom of God and made like his beloved Son is of the Lord from the beginning to its glorious consummation' (Eph. 2:8-10).

2. Salvation is of the Lord in its origination

Our Lord planned and purposed the redemption of his people from the beginning (Eph. 1:3-4; 2 Thess. 2:13). Our Lord Jesus was 'the Lamb slain from the foundation of the world' (Rev. 13:8). Salvation is too splendid and too wise to have been the product of any mind except that mind which could accomplish it.

Suppose that God had called a council of angels and declared, 'Man that I shall create will rebel against me. I shall punish all sin; my justice and my law demand that I should do so. But I intend to show mercy, for God is love! Tell me, how can my law be honoured and the demands of my justice be fulfilled that mercy may reign? Where shall mercy and truth meet together, righteousness and peace kiss each other?' (Ps. 85:10). 'How can God be just and the justifier of sinners who believe?' Those angels would still be sitting there in silence! Only God can plan and accomplish salvation (Isa. 46:9-11).

3. Salvation is of the Lord in its execution

The Father made the beloved and only begotten Son our surety, our representative and the federal head of an elect people, chosen in him and given to him to redeem and bring to glory (John 6:37-45; 10:14-16,24-31). In Adam we died; in Christ we live (Rom. 5:12; 1 Cor. 15:22). In Adam we were made sinners; in Christ we are made righteous (Rom. 5:19). In Adam we were separated from God; in Christ we are brought to God (1 Peter 3:18).

The Father is the first cause of all that took place in the work of our Redeemer. 'He [the Father] hath made him [the Son] to be sin for us [the sinner], who knew no sin [Christ was perfect]; that we might be made the righteousness of God in him [Christ]' (2 Cor. 5:21). 'It pleased the Lord to bruise him' (Isa. 53:10). Even those who planned his death, betrayed him, tried him, scourged him, nailed him to the cross and put him in the tomb did what God determined before to be done (Acts 2:22-23; 4:27-28). Christ died not as a reformer, nor as an example, nor to gain the pity of men. He died as the substitute, sin offering and sacrifice for his people. As the blood atonement on the mercy-seat of old was offered 'before the Lord', Christ Jesus, by one offering before the Lord, perfected for ever them that are sanctified (Heb 10:9-17). The Father ordained and pictured for us in the Old Testament all that our Lord would do for our redemption, and he died 'according to the scriptures' (1 Cor. 15:1-3).

4. Salvation is of the Lord in its application

'No,' says the advocate of free will, 'God has done all that he can do. He has given his Son; he has provided salvation. Now it is up to us to want it, seek it and accept it.' Can the dead sinner give himself life? Can the lost sheep find itself? Can the unregenerate beget themselves? 'Can the Ethiopian change his skin, or the leopard his spots?' (Jer. 13:23). No, my friends! His people are made willing in the day of his power. 'Of his own will begat he us with the word of truth' (James 1:18). We receive Christ and believe on his name because we are 'born of God' (John 1:12-13). Paul summed up his call in these words, found in Galatians 1:15: 'But when it pleased God, who separated me from my mother's womb, and called me by his grace, to reveal his Son in me.'

47. A fountain opened for mourners

Zechariah 12:10; 13:1

Charles Spurgeon (minister to London for thirty-eight years) wrote, 'In this scripture, first of all, there is a prophecy concerning the Jewish people; and I am happy that it confirms our hearts in the belief of the good which the Lord shall do to Israel. We know of a surety, because the Lord has said it, that the Jews will be restored to their own land and that they shall inherit the country which the Lord has given to their fathers by a covenant for ever. But, better still, they shall be converted to the faith of our Lord Jesus Christ and shall see in him that Messiah for whom their fathers looked with joyful expectation, that Redeemer of whom the prophets spoke, but who was despised and rejected by his own. Happy day, when not only the Gentiles but the Jews will be found worshipping the Lord Jesus Christ, our great Redeemer and High Priest. We have the promise, and we expect the fulfilment when the due season arrives. Israel shall own her King!'

I intend to use the text as it speaks to us, true spiritual Israel (Gal. 3:7,29); and it does speak to us on a very vital issue — repentance towards God and faith in our Lord Jesus Christ (Acts 20:20-21). One cannot have faith without repentance, nor repentance without faith; yet most repentance and true mourning over sin comes from first seeing Christ Jesus in his holiness, his power and his sacrifice. Was this not true of Isaiah (Isa. 6:1-5) and of Job? (Job 42:4-6).

It is difficult to say which is first — repentance or faith, but one writer said, 'More repentance is produced by faith than faith by repentance.' The more we see of Christ, the more we see of ourselves; and this sight produces true worship, true repentance, true faith and true salvation (John 6:40). He is worthy of the adoration and worship of those who have never sinned (as the angels). When we make him only the Saviour from sin and praise him only because he saves us from sin, we do not properly understand his lordship. He is Lord of heaven and earth! When Isaiah saw his glory, he spoke of him (John 12:41). Let's look at five divisions in these two verses of Scripture.

1. **'I will pour out upon the house of David, and upon the inhabitants of Jerusalem, the spirit of grace and of supplications'** (12:10). As I stated in the introduction, this prophecy first not only refers to the nation of Abraham, Isaac and Jacob, but also to the seed of Abraham by faith. 'He is not a Jew, which is one outwardly ... he is a Jew which is one inwardly, and circumcision is ... of the heart, in the spirit' (Rom. 2:28-29). The promise of grace and salvation was to Abraham and his seed, which is Christ and all who are in Christ by divine purpose and God-given faith (Gal. 3:16). In Christ the Father has chosen and blessed a people of every tribe, nation and tongue (Eph. 1:3-6; Rev. 7:9). All 'true Israel' shall be saved (Rom. 11:26). All that the Father has given to Christ shall be called, justified and glorified (John 6:37-39; Rom. 8:29-30). He will indeed pour out the Spirit of grace, regeneration, supplication and mercy (sure mercies) on the house of David and the inhabitants of the 'heavenly Jerusalem' (Heb. 12:22-23; Gal. 4:26).

2. **'And they shall look upon me whom they have pierced'** (12:10). Our Lord said in Isaiah 45:22, 'Look unto me, and be ye saved, all the ends of the earth: for I am God!'

I suppose when we say, 'Look to Christ,' or 'Look upon Christ,' this puzzles a lot of people. One will say, 'If Christ were in Jerusalem, I would sell up and go and look upon, and listen to, him.' Another might say, 'If Christ were here today, I would sit at his feet and look upon him.' Oh, my friends, like Nicodemus, we are bound to the flesh. 'How can I be born again, shall I enter my mother's womb?' Our saving connection with Christ has nothing to do with our natural eyes, ears and hands, but with the mind and heart. It is to hear him in the mind, look to him in the will, love and believe him in the heart.

One does not need a college degree to look! You may not be able to read, but you can look; you may be destitute of virtue, but you can look; you may have no merit, but you can look. Looking only requires my personal interest and attention. Another can pray for me, but no one can look for me: I must look to him myself. I look not to his disciples, his church, or his law; I am exhorted to look to *him* (Jer. 29:13). Salvation is in him (1 John 5:10-12).

3. **'Whom they have pierced'** (12:10). Who sent our Lord to the tree? What held him on the cross? It was not the nails, nor human weakness, nor the soldiers.

> 'Twas you, my sins, my cruel sins,
> His chief tormentors were;
> Each of my crimes became a nail,
> And unbelief the spear.
>
>   (Isaac Watts)

He *knew* no sin; it was not merely that he *had* no sin. He was acquainted with grief, but not with sin.

He was made sin for us and treated by the Father as if he were sin itself. 'Nail him to the tree, for sin must be punished; and he is numbered with the transgressors!' So when the charge is brought, 'Who crucified Christ?' I reply, 'It pleased the Father to pierce him for my sins' (Isa. 53:4-6).

4. **'And they shall mourn'** (12:10). True mourning for sin has a distinct and constant reference to the Lord Jesus. If I hate sin because I am exposed, I have not repented; I merely regret that I have been found out. If I hate sin because of judgement and hell, I have not repented; I merely regret that God is just. But if I see sin as a hateful offence against my Lord, and I see my sin as crucifying him, then I mourn with a truly broken and repentant heart (Ps. 51:3-4). True mourning is a great bitterness, as one mourns the death of his firstborn. Someone said,

> Lord, let me weep for naught but sin
> And after none but thee;
> Then I would — oh, that I might
> A constant weeper be.

A broken heart over sin is a work of the Spirit of God and will be healed (Ps. 51:17; 34:18).

5. **'In that day there shall be a fountain opened to the house of David and to the inhabitants of Jerusalem for sin and for uncleanness'** (13:1). Could this be the verse which inspired William Cowper to write that great and blessed hymn?

There is a fountain filled with blood
Drawn from Immanuel's veins;
And sinners plunged beneath that flood
Lose all their guilty stains.

Dear dying Lamb, thy precious blood
Shall never lose its power
Till all the ransomed church of God
Be saved to sin no more.'

The phrase 'in that day' can refer to several times:

That fountain was opened when God purposed to save us.
That fountain was opened to all Old Testament believers.
That fountain was opened when our Lord died.
That fountain was opened when we believed.
Thank God, that fountain will still be open in the great day of our
Lord, for we have been saved, by his grace are being saved, and our
salvation is nearer than when we believed— and the whole of the
redemptive work is because he loved us and gave himself for us
(Rev. 5:9-10).

48. The messenger of the covenant

Malachi 3:1-6

The preceding chapter (Mal. 2) is filled with rebuke and judgement against both the priests and the people for their sins. The priests were apostates from the way of the Lord and caused the people to stumble (Mal. 2:8-9). The chapter closes with these words, 'Ye have wearied the Lord with your words,' saying that the Lord takes delight in your evil ways and that there is judgement and righteousness in God. You ask, 'Where is the God of judgement?' Chapter 3 begins with the answer of our Lord to this question.

v.1. **'Behold, I will send my messenger.'** This is John the Baptist, called the last of the Old Testament prophets, who was sent to 'prepare the way' before the Lord (Isa. 40:3; John 1:6-9,23). The allusion is to kings and great men sending ambassadors before them to give notice of their coming. John said, 'I am not the Christ. I am not that prophet. I am not Elijah. I am the voice crying in the wilderness — behold the Lamb!' All of the prophets have written and preached of the Messiah's coming (Acts 10:43). Now the last of their number declares that the Messiah has been born of woman and is in the midst of them (John 1:29-34).

'**And the Lord, whom ye seek, shall suddenly come to his temple.**' The Lord Jehovah is speaking of himself, the Son of God, the promised Messiah and Christ, the Lord and Head of the church, the Redeemer of true Israel (John 4:25; Matt. 2:2-6).

Some were seeking him as a temporal deliverer, to free them from national bondage and to restore the earthly glory to Israel, but some, like Simeon, believed the Word and waited for 'thy salvation' (Luke 2:25-32).

When the Lord speaks of coming to his temple, he is actually talking about coming to the material temple in Jerusalem (the second temple — Hag. 2:1-9). The temple was built to be his, devoted to his worship, to reveal his glory and his mercy to sinners through the sacrifices and the mercy-seat. He came to that temple on several occasions (Luke 2:22-27; Mark 11:15-17; 12:35; 14:49). 'He was in the world ... and the world knew him not. He came unto his own [temple, priesthood, nation], and his own received him not' (John 1:10-11).

'Even the messenger of the covenant.' This is the covenant of grace, the everlasting covenant of which our Lord Jesus is not only the surety and mediator, but called here the messenger. He is called the messenger of that everlasting covenant of grace (Heb. 13:20-21; 7:22; 8:6) because it is revealed, made known and manifested in and through him (John 1:14; 1 John 5:20; Eph. 1: 8-10). As our King he reigns, as our Priest he perfects us and as our Prophet he reveals the mysteries of God's covenant.

'... whom ye delight in: behold he shall come.' All believers delight in him. 'Whom having not seen, ye love; in whom, though now ye see him not, yet believing, ye rejoice with joy unspeakable and full of glory' (1 Peter 1:8). And all believers delight in his covenant. David's last words on earth were words of joy and confidence in the Lord's covenant of grace (2 Sam. 23:1-5). We rejoice in the messenger of the covenant and in the covenant — its antiquity (2 Thess. 2:13), its sureness (Rom. 4:16), its immutability (Rom. 11:29), its fulness (Col. 2:9-10), its beloved messenger, surety and advocate (1 John 2:1; 1 Tim. 2:5).

v.2. **'Who may abide the day of his coming? ... Who shall stand when he appeareth?'** Who shall listen when he speaks? 'Who hath believed our report?' Isn't this not only Isaiah's question, but the question of every prophet?

> When he says, 'I and my Father are one,' who shall abide?
> When he declares, 'My kingdom is not of this world,' my kingdom is a spiritual kingdom, a kingdom of righteousness, peace and joy, who shall abide?
> When he says, 'All that my Father giveth to me shall come to me,' and 'No man can come to me except my Father draw him,' who shall abide?
> When he preaches the gospel of the cross, the tomb and the glorious resurrection as our substitute and Saviour, who shall hear?

When he talks of the new birth, eating his flesh and drinking his blood, of persecution and division caused by him, who shall abide?

'He is like a refiner's fire, and like fuller's soap.' His word is called a fire (Jer. 23:29). When it comes in power, it separates the gold from the dross, truth from error, genuine faith from false faith, and will try the works and preaching of men (1 Cor. 3:13-15). The women would boil the garments in hot water. Then they were rubbed with fuller's soap, which whitened them and took out the spots. We are sanctified by his word of truth.

v.3. **'And he shall sit as a refiner and purifier of silver.'** One can see the old refiner of precious metal. He made the fire; he knows how hot it should be; he knows when to put the metal into the fire, how long to leave it and when to take it out. All the time he sits (unalarmed and untroubled) and waits for the purifying process to do its work. Our Lord Jesus Christ has come to this earth and finished the work given to him. He is exalted at God's right hand, seated until his church is called out and his enemies are made his footstool. This verse denotes his constant care over his church from the cradle to the grave. His eye is upon them in all their ways. He will purify these **'sons of Levi'**, for they are all priests, and he will purge them that they may believe him, worship him and offer sacrifices of faith, love, praise and thanksgiving in righteousness — that is, in the righteousness of Christ (Jer. 23:5-6; 33:16). He began the work of purifying the purging, and he will finish it (Phil. 1:6).

v.4. All spiritual worship, faith, praise and offerings are acceptable to God through the Lord Jesus Christ if such are offered in the faith of his righteousness imputed and his atoning sacrifice. Without Christ, nothing we do or say is acceptable to God (Rom. 8:8; Heb. 11:6).

vv.5-6. The Lord declares that he will be **'a swift witness'** against all ungodly men and women and 'Their foot shall slide in due time' (Deut. 32:35). But as he is unchangeable in his judgements against sin, so he is unchangeable in his love and mercy to his people! Our confidence and assurance are based, not upon our faithfulness, but upon his! We are often called the **'sons of Jacob'** because, as Jacob was loved, chosen, called and blessed by the sovereign grace of God, so are we!

> All that I am, even here on earth,
> All that I hope to be,
> When Jesus comes and glory dawns,
> I owe it, Lord, to thee.

(H. Bonar, 1856)

Questions

1. The psalm of Messiah the King
1. How is the emphasis on personal free will in salvation tantamount to rejecting the rule of God?
2. What is God's response to his opponents?
3. How does the word of the sovereign God assure the success of his purpose?

2. God's two great books
1. In what other ways does creation point to the glory of God—Father, Son and Holy Spirit?
2. Why is Holy Scripture so important to our understanding of God?
3. What is to be our personal response to God's revelation of himself in his two great books?

3. The psalm of the cross
1. Spend some time thinking about 'Christ our substitute'. List some examples where Christ took our place.
2. In Matthew 27:39-44, what are the five taunts that were hurled at Christ?
3. Christ had consolation in the midst of his suffering. What was this?

4. 'The Lord is my Shepherd'
1. Why is the position of Psalm 23, following Psalm 22, significant?
2. What is the ground of the writer's certainty about his relationship to the Lord?
3. There is great consolation and contentment in knowing that 'The Lord is my shepherd.' How is this reflected in the remainder of the psalm?

5. True God, true Israel, true Redeemer

1. What misconceptions of God are corrected by a true understanding of the Lord as seen in section 1?
2. The true Israel is not a national people, but a spiritual people from every nation. What identifies the true Israel of God?
3. How has the true Redeemer earned his glory and the prize of his church? Where is his glory recognized?

6. Eight great precepts

1. We sometimes use the phrase, 'Trust in the Lord,' without much thought. How does the psalmist show what it really means to trust in the Lord?
2. When the enemies of the Lord oppose believers, why is God's sovereign power so reassuring?
3. How does an understanding of the true God help us to fulfil these eight great precepts?

7. 'My hope is in thee'

1. Have you experienced occasions when the proper course of action was to be quiet and still before God?
2. What kind of circumstances called for this response?
3. What did the experience teach you of God and of yourself?

8. 'Many, O Lord, are thy wonderful works'

1. Why might we find waiting patiently upon the Lord so difficult to put into practice?
2. What does it mean to say that Christ has saved us from a pit, established our standing and given us a new song?
3. In what ways has Christ revealed his Father to us?

9. A song of love

1. Review all Christ's kingly attributes as found in this psalm.
2. Why does the image of a sword so appropriately convey the effect of gospel preaching?
3. List and consider the blessings which fall to the King's chosen bride.

10. The sinner's prayer

1. Why is the sinner's need for mercy so foundational?
2. How can God be just to condemn sin, yet merciful to sinners?
3. Why does a knowledge of salvation produce joy?

11. 'My rock and my salvation'

1. Why is it necessary to emphasize that 'Salvation is of the Lord'?
2. In what ways will men and women try to deny the uniqueness of salvation from the Lord?
3. Why is the injunction to 'trust in him at all times' so important for us?

12. Our Lord's suffering for our sins

1. Why did Christ have to suffer?
2. For whose sins did he suffer?
3. What did this suffering achieve?

13. 'Mercy and truth are met together'

1. God has a chosen people. How does he secure their salvation?
2. If God has forgiven *all* their sin and taken away *all* his wrath, what is the status, or position, of his elect?
3. Spend some time thinking about Romans 8:28, that all things work together for good to those who love the Lord, those who are *called* according to *his* purpose.

14. The victory of the Messiah

1. What do the four names of God found in verses 1-2 reveal about God's character and nature?
2. Why does this revelation of God inspire confidence in believers?
3. List some areas where people may try to find safety or security apart from Christ. Do these provide peace? Why not?

15. 'Bless the Lord, O my soul'

1. 'As we grow in grace our prayers change.' What does this mean?
2. Why is it only God who can forgive sin?
3. Why must sinners plead for mercy rather than ask for justice?

16. 'Let the redeemed of the Lord say so'

1. May we say that all of God's providential dealings with his people are good?
2. In what respect are sinners in bondage to the law and captives of sin?
3. Can you give personal testimony to being delivered from distresses?

17. The King-Priest

1. What is the significance of Christ's sitting at the Father's right hand?

2. Compare 'Thy people shall be willing in the day of thy power' with Romans 1:16. What does this teaching reveal about free will?

3. In what ways might Melchizedek be likened to the Lord Jesus?

18. The chief cornerstone

1. Why is the mercy of God such an important element in our relationship with God?

2. Paul asks, 'Who shall lay anything to the charge of God's elect?' (Rom. 8:33). What does this teach us about the nature of justification, and why is this linked to God being on our side?

3. Why might the psalmist see this as a reason for trust and confidence in the Lord?

19. The observer and the observed

1. How does God's intimate knowledge of you make you feel?

2. The psalmist regards as precious God's thoughts of him. Why?

3. God will judge the wicked. How does this reconcile with a God of love?

20. 'Praise the Lord, O my soul'

1. Why ought we to be circumspect in our approach to, and addressing of, God?

2. What assurance can be drawn from the psalmist's emphasis on the LORD, Jehovah?

3. Why is a Christian's hope in Christ more of a certainty than a mere possibility?

21. Wisdom in Christ

1. What may we learn about the opportunity and location for gospel preaching?

2. God has a particular love for those who are chosen to salvation. How is this love demonstrated in Christ? (cf. Rom. 5:8).

3. As he is eternally one with the Father, Christ's glory is immeasurable. How should this thought influence, first, our worship, and then our witness, of him?

22. The conclusion of the whole matter
1. Why will academic achievement, the pursuit of pleasure and ambitious schemes ultimately prove a spiritually barren exercise?
2. Does this mean that such interests are wrong?
3. What may we learn about priorities from this passage? (Consider also Matthew 6:33).

23. 'Remember now thy Creator'
1. Remembering God means remembering the Triune God in all three persons. Why is this so?
2. Recognition of the frailty of our being directs us to fear God and obey his Word. Why?
3. Do you think there is a link between this emphasis on worshipping God in youth and the great pressures placed on young people by the world?

24. 'My beloved is mine and I am his'
1. Why is Solomon's love song so apt to describe the relationship between Christ and the church?
2. Why might the church be so confident in her relationship with Christ?
3. What images of future consummation of this love relationship have we of heaven?

25. 'What is thy beloved more than another beloved?'
1. Consider some of the world's loves and how they displace Christ.
2. Why can a Christian testify to Christ's superiority over all other loves?
3. List the superlatives which Christ brings to his people.

26. 'Come now and let us reason together'
1. What is total depravity?
2. Given that this condition is true, why is the verse, 'Salvation is of the Lord' (Jonah 2:9), so meaningful?
3. Since God calls us to reason about our lost condition, what might we expect if we despise his call?

27. 'Here am I; send me'
1. What was Isaiah's lasting impression of his vision of Christ?

2. What was the prophet's personal response to this sight of splendour and majesty?
3. How is the subsequent administering of the live coal a type of God's mercy to a sinner through the gospel?

28. Jesus Christ — the mighty God
1. Why is revelation of the essence of the incarnation?
2. Why is the birth of Christ by a virgin an essential aspect of the incarnation?
3. What do Christ's wonderful names tell us about his purpose in taking a human body?

29. The day of divine visitation
1. Do you have personal experience of a day of divine visitation when the Lord revealed mercy in Christ to you?
2. How has that revelation altered or converted you?
3. Do you think there is a danger is encouraging unbelievers to partake of 'family fare'?

30. The believer's comfort
1. Who are the Lord's people? What does it mean to be chosen, called, redeemed and believing?
2. Why should redeemed people need to be comforted?
3. What comfort have we when we behold our God? Consider particularly the quotation from John Gill.

31. The Messiah
1. In what sense can Christ be said to be elect of God — 'mine elect'?
2. What is the significance of the Lord's words on the cross, 'It is finished,' in the context of the accomplishment of redemption for the elect?
3. How has Christ magnified God's law?

32. A just God and a Saviour
1. What does the fact that God hides himself as Saviour tell us of the timing of our salvation?
2. Yet God has not spoken in secret. How has God revealed himself to the people of this world?
3. What makes the general revelation of God as Saviour effectual for the elect?

33. The Redeemer describes himself
1. How might preachers today 'make man to be more than he is and God to be less that he is'?
2. In what way does Christ's prophetic office warn us about the false witness of cults and sects? (cf. Heb. 1:1-2)
3. Why do Christians enjoy such a sure hope and joyful confidence in the success of Christ's work?

34. Our confession of faith
1. What indicates that Isaiah knew the necessity of Holy Spirit power to make gospel preaching effectual in the soul of a sinner?
2. What does the description of our Lord as a 'man of sorrows and acquainted with grief' tell us about his time on earth?
3. Why are substitution and satisfaction so crucial to an understanding of the gospel?

35. 'Seek ye the Lord'
1. Why do men spend time, energy and strength in pursuing false works religion?
2. As the mercies of God in Christ are preached, what is God's promise to those who come believing?
3. What does believing in Christ actually mean?

36. The person and work of the Messiah
1. What does the Lord do for those who are heartbroken by soul-binding sin?
2. Having released the captive sinner, what does our Lord then give?
3. What does the provision of these benefits achieve?

37. The Lord our righteousness
1. The image of a wolf made to look like a sheep tells us that false teachers may not be easily discerned. How are true Christians to identify such deceivers?
2. Does it matter what kind of gospel is preached in our churches? Why?
3. What is the meaning of this statement: 'Election is not salvation; it is unto salvation'?

38. The believer's hope
1. Why might a sinner's natural condition be described as hopeless?

2. Where might such a sinner find a source of hope in the midst of despair?

3. Summarize the six reasons why a sinner may trust Christ.

39. From nothing to everything

1. How depraved is totally depraved, and what does this amount to for sinners?

2. How has God met the resultant need in depraved sinners?

3. What has been the effect of God's grace upon such men and women?

40. Lost, driven away, broken, sick

1. Compare the role of a shepherd with that of a preacher/pastor. What lessons may we draw?

2. What is the principal duty of a Christian minister?

3. What is the essence of such a ministry?

41. 'Can these bones live?'

1. 'The dead sinner cannot ... believe because he is devoid of spiritual life,' yet we are called to repent and believe the gospel. How is this possible?

2. What does the phrase, 'free and sovereign grace', mean?

3. What is the means employed by God to call his people to himself? What message ought we then to insist upon being preached?

42. Four things God taught Nebuchadnezzar

1. Why do many people have so low a view of the living God today?

2. How might we learn of the true greatness and glory of God?

3. What will be the effect in our lives of a growing understanding of God?

43. 'Thy God will deliver thee'

1. What does Daniel's conduct reveal about the kind of man he was?

2. How do we measure against God's holy law?

3. How has God dealt with the problem of our law-breaking?

44. Hosea — a type of Christ

1. How has God demonstrated his love towards his chosen people?

2. What does Hosea's care of Gomer in her rebellious state tell us of God's dealings with us in our rebellious condition?

3. What do Hosea's experiences reveal about Christ's labour of love for us?

45. A famine to be feared
1. Israel at various times suffered famine, captivity and military occupation. Why is a 'famine of the hearing of the Word of God' so serious?
2. What evidences of this famine of hearing are present in churches today?
3. Are there personal and collective safeguards we may take against such a spiritual famine?

46. Salvation is of the Lord
1. What do we mean by the words, 'Salvation is of the Lord'?
2. How may we know that salvation was no divine afterthought?
3. How may we be sure that the execution and application of salvation will satisfy a holy God?

47. A fountain opened for mourners
1. Why are repentance and faith so closely intertwined in Scripture?
2. What is the difference between repentance and regret?
3. What is the source of true spiritual repentance for sin?

48. The messenger of the covenant
1. Why is Christ's title of messenger of the covenant so apt?
2. Why is Christ the reason for joy and delight on the part of believers?
3. What is involved for Christians in Christ's work of refining and purifying?